Self-Actualized by Poker:

The Path from Categorical Learning to Free-Thinking

By Roman Gelperin

Self-Actualized by Poker: The Path from Categorical Learning to
Free-Thinking, by Roman Gelperin

Visit the author's website at: www.RomanGelperin.com

Copyright © 2019 Roman Gelperin

ISBN: 9781687839893

Table of Contents

Introduction

There is a term in philosophy that nine out of ten individuals never even heard, yet on which nearly all their fulfillment in life, efficacy at work, and growth toward psychological health depends. This term is "epistemology." Epistemology means, to quote one famous philosopher: "the method by which [a person] acquires and organizes [his] knowledge." In other words, it is one's method of thinking.

We humans are born with a mind, but no instructions about the right way to use it. This correct method must either be discovered or learned, anew, by each individual—or remain unknown to him. The same way a person must learn to drive a car, so must the person learn how to use his mind—to obtain information from the external (and internal) world, process it, and end up with a repertoire of accurate knowledge about reality.

If he doesn't use the correct method, he will tend to acquire—and thus make his decisions, reason, and act on—not valuable truths, but dangerous falsehoods. And though this usually leads only to a general, diffuse uncertainty in life; to uninspired, mediocre performance at work; and to a base level of conflict with oneself, other people, and existence; it can sometimes result in profound tragedy. That is, however, the unfortunate case with most people.

The title of this book, *Self-Actualized by Poker*, draws on a concept coined by the great humanistic psychologist Abraham Maslow. A self-actualized person, according to Maslow, was one who had reached the highest level of psychological health. Operationally defined, this meant (at a minimum) that he was totally free of internal conflicts (completely at peace with himself, and with no insecurities, shame, or guilt), while also experiencing a near-constant joy, pleasure, and satisfaction in living—all sustained over a period of many months or years. Maslow studied these remarkable people, and he discovered in them a unique psychological syndrome (a collection of character traits that often occurred together). Not only were these individuals free of internal conflicts, not only did they derive massive enjoyment from life (frequently punctuated by moments of intense happiness, ecstasy, bliss), they also possessed many other exceptional qualities of human beings at their highest potential.

They were supremely confident in themselves, in their thinking, and in their decisions. They were almost flawlessly honest, extremely spontaneous in their actions, and displayed an effortless, natural creativity in almost everything they did. They were incredibly independent, self-motivated, and self-determining. They could serenely withstand even the worst blows of misfortune, and remain happy while facing even the harshest external conditions. All of them, without an exception, had some important, meaningful, higher purpose in life — some cherished life's work, which they were successfully and passionately pursuing. Yet the main characteristic all this was built on, and revolved around, was this: a correct — or at least mostly correct — epistemology!

There occur certain incredible moments in some people's lives, moments so positive and pregnant with meaning that they can forever transform one's whole personality structure, behavior, and worldview, in a matter of hours. Maslow called these outstanding moments "peak-experiences" — meaning, moments of extremely intense positive emotion.

Among these, there is a specific *type* of peak-experience, which I call the "intellectual peak-experience:" in other words, a moment of highly intense positive emotion produced by a major insight or realization. These often are moments of sudden enlightenment, of breakthroughs in understanding, of earth-shattering revelation. They can, in a flash, illuminate a huge swath of existence, granting the person sight — the clear sight of conscious understanding — where before there was only darkness. And because real understanding frequently also bestows one with power — the power to pass judgment, to teach, and to act on that understanding — as well as the inspiration to put one's discovery into practice, it's not so surprising that such an experience can transform a person's whole character, intellect, and path in life in a big way.

And among these experiences, there exists another, more specific *subtype* of intellectual peak-experience, which I call the "epistemology experience:" meaning, a moment of highly intense positive emotion produced by a very specific insight or realization, in which the person discovers the correct—or a large part of the correct—epistemology. This is a completely unique and unmistakable peak-experience, which gives the individual not just a new understanding of some part of the world, but the basic ability to independently reach such an understanding of any part of the world he puts his mind to. It's also one of the most powerful, far-reaching, and transformative experiences available to a human being—and one we commonly find in the lives of self-actualized people.

It was, in fact, a crucial defining experience—if not *the* crucial defining experience—in the lives of many prominent self-actualizers, including (1) the legendary theoretical physicist, Albert Einstein, (2) the father of humanistic psychology, Abraham Maslow, (3) the ingenious novelist and philosopher, Ayn Rand, (4) the renowned Russian writer, historian, and Nobel Prize winner, Aleksandr Solzhenitsyn, (5) the great 19th century German philosopher, Friedrich Nietzsche, and (6) the legendary Hollywood actor and martial artist, Bruce Lee. Each of these persons independently reported having a major, life-changing epistemology experience, which restructured their psyches, passions, and courses in life permanently, and made them the world-movers they would ultimately become. A transformation like this, of course, is always extremely astounding, but it does make intuitive sense. After all, once one's fundamental method of thinking changes, one's entire relationship to oneself and the external world has to change along with it.

This book is a detailed account of my own epistemology experience, attained through a multi-year effort of trying to master the game of poker. It was, indeed, the single most important, definitive few hours of my life. And, as might be expected, everything changed!

I originally intended this book to be the first several chapters in a much larger work titled *Self-Actualizing People in History: Four*

Biographies and a Memoir, where I thoroughly investigated the biographies of four self-actualizing individuals—Abraham Maslow, Aleksandr Solzhenitsyn, Ayn Rand, and Albert Einstein—as well as my own parallel life-experiences, as a rigorous demonstration of what's really required to achieve self-actualization. Since the epistemology experience played a key role in every one of these people's lives, I felt it imperative to include a full description of my own experience—written to be the most complete, detailed, comprehensive account of an epistemology experience in all literature—to show exactly what it entailed, and thus to inform the rest of the book.

Although it did go rather deeply into the technical aspects of poker, and included a fair deal of math (albeit only at a middle school level), I figured that any intelligent reader would be willing and able to put in the effort required to learn the technical details, and grasp the mathematical parts, to reap the transcendent reward contained in those chapters. Then, I gave the nearly finished manuscript to read to a close friend of mine, and found that despite her very best efforts, and being a highly intelligent person, she simply wasn't able to understand any of the math. She later turned out to have a condition known as dyscalculia (a learning disability that is the mathematical equivalent of dyslexia), without being aware that she had it. But this led to a major shift in my perspective.

I then realized that there was a substantial population of otherwise intelligent readers, who—whether resulting from dyscalculia, a terrible public-school education, or something else entirely—were simply unable to understand math at a middle school level. This would render the lion's share of my larger book, which contained zero math, but an abundance of psychological wisdom they could greatly benefit from, pretty much inaccessible to this group of readers.

So, I decided to severely abridge this section in the larger work—culling out most of the math and finer details of poker—and publish the full version instead in a separate book: this one. That way, the readers not willing or able to work through a hundred pages of poker and math to get to the heart of the larger book, could still access all of the valuable insights in *Self-Actualizing People in History.* And the readers willing to put in the effort to derive the maximum benefit, can find the full narrative here, and obtain the most complete understanding of the epistemology experience.

That said, for any reader who wishes to put in the mental work, this book—*Self-Actualized by Poker*—will teach him the single most important concept a human being needs to know: What is the correct way to use one's mind? What isn't? And what paths one can take to unlock that correct understanding within oneself. To that end, I also appended a couple additional sections at the end of this book (see Appendices A and B), to further clarify and expand upon this vital concept. And having myself had the epistemology experience, I can attest, there is no understanding more crucial for living a life of joy and well-being, escaping from psychological misery, and achieving one's fullest human potential than this!

Part One: The Categorical Player

There were two major experiences in my life that were by far the most important in directing its course, and which eventually led me to self-actualization (the highest level of psychological health available to a human being).

The first occurred at the age of sixteen when, in a sudden moment of enlightenment, after re-reading a poker book for the third time, I discovered what was, at least for me, a completely novel method of thinking. It struck me at the time as self-evident that this new type of thought was exactly what the human mind was designed for; and it was an utter mystery to me why, until that very moment, I hadn't the slightest inkling that my mind could be used in this way. I called this new method of thought free-thinking or true-thinking, and it has served as my guiding light ever since. My second key experience occurred roughly two-and-a-half years later, when at the age of nineteen, I sustained a serious injury to my spine that rendered me unable to walk, at least not without excruciating pain, for about one year.

This book is a detailed account of that first experience.

I was lying on the bed in my room, in my parent's sixth floor apartment in Brooklyn, New York. I was then in my third year of high school. The book I was reading, now for the third time, was the third volume in a quite successful series of books for poker players titled *Harrington on Hold'em*.

I had already been playing poker avidly for the past two years, having first been introduced to it through the petty games held at and after school among a few friends—and I soon became determined to get good at the game. Since that time in my freshman year of high school, I had read over a dozen poker books, including the first two volumes of *Harrington on Hold'em*, and assimilated their contents with ease. I began playing online too, and was winning reliably. At that point and for many months prior, I had been spending the lion's share of each day playing and studying poker. I considered myself somewhat of an expert. I was certainly the best player, by far, at my school. And I was seriously entertaining the idea of a career as a professional poker player.[1]

But this new book baffled me. I had read it twice before and was simply unable to understand the ideas it contained. There was a good reason for this, for this book wasn't like any I had ever encountered. It described and attempted to teach a process of decision-making that was completely different from the one I'd been playing poker with, and indeed living my whole life with, until then. That initial mode of thinking that this book would soon wean me off of was categorization: Its essence was to treat each individual situation, whether in poker or in real life, as an instance of one *category* or another, and to select the course of action in that instance based on what the category it fit into prescribed. The substitute this book offered was to treat each dealt hand in poker as a *unique* situation, with its own unique determinants, and to base one's decision in it on the *individual analysis* of those determinants.[2]

This is a difficult concept to understand, especially if one has no experience with it, so I will try to explain it as meticulously as I can. First, I want to make perfectly clear what a category is and how it applies to the game of poker. For the sake of consistency, I will only be talking throughout this book about Texas Hold'em—although I did

---

[1] For those readers who have the conception of poker as being a game based entirely on luck—like lottery or craps or roulette—in which "the house always wins" in the end, and all skill and strategy is simply the delusion of crazed gamblers, I urge you to abandon that notion now. Poker is a game that combines luck and skill, in which a player competes not against "the house," but against other players. Skillful gameplay and sound strategy give the adept player a definite edge against his weaker, less-skilled opponents, and make him a reliable winner over them in the long run. In essence, a good player has to get less lucky to win than his weaker opponents, and this adds up to a steady profit over time.

[2] Poker players alternately use the term "hand" to sometimes refer just to the cards a player is holding, and other times to the entire situation at the table and how it unfolds during one dealt hand (in the cards sense). The meaning used in each case should be self-evident.

also play other forms of poker, this was the game I specialized in and devoted the most time to learning.[3]

CATEGORIES IN POKER

1.) What is a category? A category is a mental folder for classifying and grouping many individual items into a single unit. (The word "giraffe," for example, is a category that groups together all individual giraffes.) A category is defined by a specific set of characteristics that each of the items it seeks to classify may or may not possess. ("Giraffe," once again, may be defined as: a large, non-extinct, quadrupedal mammal, with stubby horns, hooved feet, and a very long neck about the size of its body.) If an item possesses every one of those characteristics, it can be said to belong in that category. If it is missing even one of those characteristics, then it doesn't belong in that category. Using this process of categorization, we can group together sets of similar items that all share certain definite characteristics.[4]

The defining attributes of a category can vary, depending on the person using that category, and the goal he seeks to accomplish in doing so. Still, because a category is a mental tool, and the items he seeks to categorize have their own independent reality, some definitions will accomplish his goal better than others. (If, as we might assume, a person using the category "giraffe" wants it to include every giraffe in the world, he must choose his definition carefully. If he defines "giraffe" as: a large, yellow, non-extinct, quadrupedal mammal, with a very long neck and brown spots, this wouldn't be an accurate

---

[3] If you're not familiar with the rules of Texas Hold'em, I highly recommend looking them up. (I've included the complete rules to the game in Appendix C of this book.) It only takes a few minutes to learn, and will greatly help you to understand the upcoming discussion.

[4] I use the term "items" very broadly here, because essentially anything can be categorized. Objects, actions, movements, environments, situations, and so forth, can all be items subject to categorization. Really, anything that possesses discernable characteristics, which is essentially everything in existence, can be categorized.

definition. It would be too narrow, since it excludes albino giraffes — which are white rather than yellow with brown spots — from that category. If he, on the other hand, defined "giraffe" as: a large, non-extinct, quadrupedal, hooved mammal native to Africa, this also would be an inferior definition. It would be too broad, since it includes zebra, antelope, gazelle, and other African ungulates within the same category.)

This categorical arrangement by similarity has numerous uses for thinking, decision making, and communication that are too vast to enumerate here. But I will list a few.

For one, categorization allows us, if we so choose, to treat all the items contained in a category as a single entity: the category. This is useful for contemplating the significance of a multitude of individual items at once (if, for instance, we wished to ponder the role of giraffes in the African ecosystem). This is especially helpful to us humans who, as psychological studies have shown, can keep a maximum of just seven to nine separate items — at any one time — in our working memory.

Categorization also gives us the ability to treat a variety of different items as if they were identical. This is particularly useful if we seek to isolate only the important characteristics of those items and disregard the rest. (If we wished to compare the feeding behavior of different animals, for example, we could state that giraffes are herbivorous ruminants — animals that chew, regurgitate, and re-chew their cud — with zero regard for the color, age, location, height, or gender of those giraffes.)

Finally, categorization makes it easy for us to convey a massive amount of information at once. With just a single word, the *name* of a category, we can label an item as belonging to that category, and thereby instantly provide another person with a very specific idea of that item and the various characteristics it possesses — something that would surely be very tedious if we had to describe each of those attributes separately. (When we call an animal a "giraffe," for example, assuming the person we're talking to knows the word, and has about the same definition of it as we do, this transmits to him a large catalog of its attributes—the long neck, stubby horns, hooved feet, and so on—without us having to list all of them one by one.)

A vital facet of categorization, which is a big reason why it's so useful, is that categories can be divided (or broken down) into smaller, more specific sub-categories. Each sub-category is defined by all the same characteristics as the larger category, plus some additional ones.[5] (In the case of "giraffe," this category can be divided into the four extant species of giraffe: the Northern giraffe, the Southern giraffe, the Somali giraffe, and the Masai giraffe; or, if we wanted, into male and female giraffes; or, if we wanted, into giraffes at the Bronx Zoo, giraffes at the Boston Zoo, giraffes in the African wilderness, and so on.) These sub-categories can of course have their own sub-categories, which can in turn have their own, and so forth. In this way, we are able to create a system of telescoping categories, ranging from very general categories to very specific ones, in which one general super-ordinate category subsumes a great multitude of increasingly more specific sub-ordinate categories.

As a rule: The more general a category, the fewer characteristics it is defined by, the more items can be grouped into that category, and the less information it provides about those items. The more specific a category, the more characteristics it is defined by, the fewer items can be grouped into it, and the more information it will provide about those items. ("Giraffe," for example, conveys more information than "mammal," and less information than "Northern giraffe.")

A category can become more and more specific and subsume less and less items until its defining characteristics are so numerous and specific that it will contain only a single item (for instance, female giraffes at the Bronx zoo with a heart-shaped spot on their left hindquarters). At that point, the category is reduced to the individual item it seeks to classify, and the category becomes moot. To consider unique

---

[5] Of course, characteristics can also have different levels of detail: for example, the general "green" versus the more specific "dark green." But this is the same as saying that the characteristic "dark green" is actually two characteristics: "green" plus "dark."

items individually, we no longer require classification, only identifi-
cation: that is, to simply observe and identify the various attributes of
a given item. Then, a proper name, rather than a category, can be
adopted to refer to that item (such as "Mindy the giraffe").

2.) How does this apply to poker? There are two types of item that players
usually seek to categorize when playing poker. The first of these items
is the "hand," and this applies to both the player's own hand and the
(possible) hands of his opponents. The hand is either a player's two
hidden cards before the flop, or the best five-card combination of
those two cards and the board-cards after the flop. Preflop, the individual hands A-A, K-K, and Q-Q may be grouped into the category of
"large pairs."[6] Hands like A-K, A-Q, A-J, K-Q, K-J, and so on, may be
classified as "high cards." By convention, players usually classify
hands like 8-7 suited and 7-6 suited as "suited connectors." And players often group all ragged hands like J-4, Q-7, T-6, and so on under the
category of "junk" or "trash" hands. Of course, what a player chooses
to consider large pairs, high cards, trash, and so on, is left to his own
discretion.

    After the flop, hands are almost by necessity classified according
to rank. For instance, on a board of K-6-2, a hand with a king in it
(other than K-K, K-6, or K-2) can now be classified as top pair, any
hand with a six (other than 6-6, K-6, or 6-2) as middle pair, any hand
with a two (other than 2-2, K-2, or 6-2) as bottom pair, and so forth.
The rules of poker make this kind of classification almost compulsory,
since the winner of a pot is determined by who has the highest-rank-
ing hand, and top pair will always beat middle pair, and middle pair
will always beat bottom pair, and so on. Accordingly, since flushes
and straights are high ranking hands that beat any pair, two pair, or
three of a kind, hands that contain four cards of a single suit or four

---

[6] The notation I'm using here is the standard poker notation for denoting
a two-card Hold'em hand. All cards Ace to Ten are denoted by their first
letter (i.e. K for King), and all cards Nine to Two are denoted by their
number. Hence, A-A means Ace-Ace, J-T means Jack-Ten, Q-6 means
Queen-Six, and 5-3 means Five-Three.

cards in a row (before all five cards on the board are dealt) are classified as flush-draws and straight-draws, respectively.

These classifications are useful for *thinking* about the game, specifically because they allow a player to regard all hands of a certain type
as a single entity. And this can be extremely practical. If a player has
Q-Q on a flop of K-8-3, for instance, *all* top pairs (his biggest worry on
such a flop) beat him, and *all* middle pairs and bottom pairs (and no
pairs) are losing to him. It does not make much difference, if his opponent has top pair, what that opponent's actual (individual) hand
is—whether his exact two cards are A-K, or K-2, or anything in between, since any hand that has a King in it (other than K-K) has an
almost identical winning percentage against him (with only slight de-
viations of a few percent more or less).[7] Accordingly, a player can simplify his thinking in this hand to: "What chance is there that the
opponent has a King? And how do I play my hand so that I lose the
least amount of money when he does have that top pair, and win the
most when he only has a middle or a bottom pair (or an even worse
hand)?"

In many hands, a player often has to consider additional possibilities, including that the opponent has a flush, a flush draw, a straight,
a straight draw, overcards, underpairs, trips, two-pair, a full house,
and so on. But those too are categorized *types* of hands. And by thinking in terms of these hand categories, a player can reduce the 55
unique hands that give his opponent four cards to a flush to the single
category of "flush draw,"[8] just as he reduces the 132 unique hands that
give his opponent a pair of kings in the previous example to the single

---

[7] K-8 and K-3 also have an almost identical percent chance of winning
against QQ, even though they really make two-pair.

[8] With two cards of a given suit, let's say diamonds, on the board, and two
cards of that suit in the opponent's hand, out of the remaining 11 cards of
that suit still hidden (13 in total minus the 2 on the board), the opponent
has [11*10]/2—for a total of 55—possible combinations of two diamond
cards he can have in his hand.

category of "top pair."[9] Even on the most complex and dangerous boards (where straight draws, flush draws, two-pairs, sets, and so forth all need to be taken into serious consideration), a player will virtually always be able to reduce to just five or six possible categories, each with a certain consistent winning percentage, the 1081 unique hand combinations that the opponent can actually hold.[10]

Preflop hand categories, by the way, (such as large pairs, small pairs, high cards, suited connectors, and so on) are also groups of hands that share a consistent winning percentage—at least against other such groups of hands.[11] This is why they are useful.

The pivotal point that the reader must not miss here is that the above type of categorization, which treats groups of similar individual hands as single entities, serves the primary purpose of helping a poker player *think* about a situation. It allows him to simultaneously weigh all the hundreds of concrete, individual possibilities by consolidating them into just a handful of abstract, general possibilities. Notice that each category of hand is designated by a unique name (top pair, flush draw, etc.)—this name can be used to refer to all the individual hands subsumed under a category at once, and that of course

---

[9] On a board of K-8-3, the number of possible card combinations with which the opponent can have a king in his hand, but not specifically K-K (we are including K-8 and K-3 here), is 3*44—the three remaining kings times the forty-four remaining unknown cards that aren't also kings (our own two queens and the three open board cards are *known* cards that we know the opponent can't hold)—making a total of 132.

[10] If we are talking about the flop, there are five known cards (the three on the board and two in your hand), leaving 47 unknown cards. Out of those, the opponent can have [47*46]/2—for a total of 1081—different individual hands. (We divide by two because the order in which he's dealt the cards doesn't matter: Ace-King being the same as King-Ace.)

[11] All low pocket pairs, for example, will have about a 19% chance of winning against large pocket pairs, and about a 54% chance of winning against high cards; while suited connectors will have about a 40% chance of winning against high cards, and a 22% chance against large pocket pairs.

greatly facilitates the person's ability to think of that category as a single entity.

Now, there is a second kind of item poker players will often seek to categorize, and that is the entire current situation at the table (including the player's own hand) during the present betting round. This categorization does not provide any benefit for helping the player think, but it does allow him to instantly reach a decision for how to *act* (that is, whether to fold, call, or raise) in that situation.

Every competent poker player knows that merely knowing the rank of one's own hand (whether it is top pair, or middle pair, and so on) is not nearly enough information for making a prudent poker decision. Before making a decision, a good player will often take into account a multitude of other factors, including the amount of money in the pot, the round of betting it is currently on, the texture of the board, the number of opponents in the hand, the player's position in relation to those opponents, the previous betting action, and—of course—the two cards the player holds and how they match up with the board cards. Clearly, scrutinizing all of these factors and weighing them against each other is hard work. It can be very dubious work, too, if the player isn't certain how much weight to give to one factor or another. This is where categorization can become very useful.

Over the course of play, many situations will come up that are very similar to one another. Thus, after a player determines what the correct play is in one situation, he will soon notice that similar situations arise in which the same play is correct for the same reasons. These similar situations, which share the same critical determinants and therefore lead to the same decision, can be put into a single category. Then, all the player needs to do is recognize when a situation falls into that category, and he will instantly know the correct play to make in it. He will no longer have to go through the same lengthy process of reasoning to solve the same basic problem when it comes up anew: He just needs to recognize that this is a problem he has already solved before, and so apply his past solution to this current problem.

An experienced poker player, who has seen and determined the correct play (or at least what he thinks is the correct play) in a large variety of situations, will inevitably be able to recognize many different types (or categories) of situation, and thus immediately know which play to make in each of them. A player who has a large collection of such categories and their corresponding "correct plays" memorized can effectively automate his decision-making process during the game. Playing poker will then become for him much less an exercise in reasoning and much more an exercise in recognition; which is, by the way, something that the human mind is extremely efficient at, and normally capable of accomplishing within a split second.

I finally want to call the reader's attention to the distinct relationship that exists between the first kind of category we discussed, that which allows a player to treat a group of individual hands as a single entity, and this second type that allows him to instantly know which decision to make in a certain situation. The first has its main utility in *thinking*: It helps simplify the player's reasoning process in deciding the correct way to play a hand. The second categorizes the conclusion he reaches as a *result* of that reasoning process and, basically, standardizes it.

Incidentally, the categories of this second type *do not* have their own unique names. Each category of situation is designated only by its defining characteristics. For instance: Holding "top-pair on a ragged queen-high flop with no flush possibilities, against one opponent who called your preflop raise from the big blind and who now checks to you on the flop" is one distinct category of situation, and there is no shortened way to refer to it. However, a player never actually needs to *refer* to the situation at all (at least not while playing). He needs only to recognize that it is a type of situation in which he already knows the correct play, and then simply make that play. To label each type of situation with its own name would only be a waste of effort. And since so many different types of situation can come up in a poker game, a player would likely need well over a hundred different names to refer to them all.

MY POKER BEGINNINGS, RIGID RULES, AND
RATIONALIZATION

We can now return, finally, to my personal experience with the game. I learned to play poker in precisely the categorical way I just described: I would think in terms of hand categories and would make decisions according to the "correct play" that each category of situation prescribed. As I mentioned, I initially learned how to play and think about poker from books. My categorical approach to the game was shaped in part by the nature of those books, and in part by my own category-centered mode of thinking at the time. Recall, that it was freeing myself from this categorical mode of thinking that would become one of the great defining moments of my life.

Every one of the poker books I initially read was authored or co-authored by a successful, sometimes tremendously successful, professional poker player who had made hundreds of thousands and sometimes millions of dollars skillfully playing the game. All of these books proclaimed the goal of making the reader into a winning poker player, by teaching him the way that the book's author(s) played and approached the game. Here are a few excerpts:

> We [the authors] believe that this book will be instrumental in improving the play of many players who wish to have better success in middle limit holdem games. . . . We are sure you will receive a poker education from us that will make middle limit holdem games a nice source of profit for you.

> Whatever your level of play, the succeeding chapters will introduce you to theories and concepts of poker that will eliminate your reliance on luck and lead you to become an expert who relies on his skills.

> *This book picks up where the beginners' books leave off.* We aim to teach you how to transform yourself from a good player to an expert and from a modest winner to a big winner. We want to

teach you to squeeze every last penny of value out of your games. To help you do this, we introduce some advance concepts that you have likely never before considered. In fact, some of them have never before appeared in print.

This was all very enticing, of course, and I eagerly took to reading these books in hopes that I too would be able to make a truckload of money playing poker. The books certainly did their job, and I did become a winning poker player. The way they did this, however, was by supplying me with a strict set of categories to play by—each one dictating a predetermined "correct" play for a particular type of situation.

For the *preflop* part of the game, for example, virtually every instructional poker book directly provided a comprehensive categorical system of decision-making that prescribed a certain "correct" play for almost every preflop situation that could arise. Since there were a very limited number of these, only a couple dozen categories were required to cover all the possibilities. To quote one book: "In Texas hold'em it is relatively easy to specify exactly how the first two cards should be played. This is because at this stage of play, proper strategy is not yet that complicated." The book *Small Stakes Hold'em: Winning Big with Expert Play*, for instance, provided an elegant chart of guidelines for exactly how to play in every possible preflop scenario, depending on your position in the hand, the cards you hold, and the action in front of you (pictured below):

Early Position *The first three seats to the left of the blinds*	Middle Position *The three seats to the left of early position*	Late position *One off the button and the button*	Small Blind	Big Blind
If there is no raise *Play:* AA-77, any two suited cards ten or higher (e.g., AKs, QTs, etc.), AK-AJ, and KQ *Raise [with]:* AA-TT, AKs-AJs, and AK-AQ	**If there is no raise** *Play:* Any pocket pair, AKs-A2s, KQs-K9s, QJs-Q9s, JTs-J9s, T9s-98s, AK-AT, and KQ-KJ *Raise [with]:* AA-99, AKs-ATs, KQs-KJs, AK-AJ, and KQ	**If there is no raise** *Play:* Same hands that you would play from *middle position* plus 87s-54s and any two offsuit cards ten or higher. *Raise [with]:* AA-99, AKs-A8s, KQs-KTs, QJs, AK-AT, and KQ	**If there is no raise** *Play:* Same hands that you would play from *late position*, plus any two suited cards. *Raise [with]:* AA-99, AK-ATs, KQs-KJs, and AK-AQ	**If there is raise** *Raise [wi* Same ha that you wo raise from small blind
Against a Raise *Play:* AA-TT, AKs-AJs, KQs, and AK *Reraise:* AA-TT, AKs, and AK	**Against a Raise** Same guidelines that you would use from *early position* against a raise	**Against a Raise** Same guidelines that you would use from *early and middle position* against a raise, except that if three players have entered the pot so far (the raiser and at least two callers) also call with any pocket pair and QJs-T9s	**Against a Raise** Same guidelines that you would use from *early position* against a raise, except add all pocket pairs (as long as one player besides the raiser has also entered the pot).	**Against a R** *Play:* Sa hands that would play f *late* position one bet, ex remove weak off hands, AT, KT, QJ-QT, JT. This lea any pocket p many su hands, AK and KQ. *Reraise:* AA AKs, and AK
Against a raise and a Reraise *Play:* AA-QQ and AKs *Raise:* AA-QQ and AKs	**Against a raise and a Reraise** *Play:* AA-QQ and AKs *Raise:* AA-QQ and AKs	**Against a raise and a Reraise** *Play:* AA-QQ and AKs *Raise:* AA-QQ and AKs	**Against a raise and a Reraise** *Play:* AA-QQ and AKs *Raise:* AA-QQ and AKs	**Against a ra and a Rerais** *Play:* AA- and AKs *Raise:* AA- and AKs

(These were actually the guidelines for a standard "tight" game, where 3 to 5 play on average see the flop. For a "loose" game, where 6-8 players see the flop on avera the book provided another, similar table with slightly altered guidelines.)

"If you are new to hold'em you should memorize the[se] hand rankings and how to play the first two cards. We see no better way to master this area of play," said one book. Of course, the author of these guidelines took special care to disclaim that "*These recommendations are not rigid,*" and instead suggested to "View them like training wheels for preflop play: When you feel lost, look to these guidelines for a decent *default* play." He also noted that "An expert player who fully understands preflop and postflop concepts will frequently deviate (correctly) from these suggestions."

But such warnings were, at least at first, absolutely lost on me. Given the categorical mindset I had at the time, I was more than content to follow these categorical guidelines to the letter.

As for a similar set of categorical guidelines for *postflop* play, the books took a different approach to providing this. Unlike the very limited number of preflop situations, there are so many different postflop scenarios that could occur that it would have taken hundreds of separate categories to cover them all. "After the first round," one of the books stated, "the game quickly becomes so complex that it is impossible to discuss every situation." "Which is why," it continued, "it's important to develop general strategic concepts to guide you toward winning play." Thus, the books attempted to teach a variety of these general concepts and strategies, which the reader could apply to any postflop situation in order to arrive at the correct play, without categorically covering every eventuality.

The most common implement these books used to teach the reader postflop play—and virtually every book used this—was the medium of *practice hands,* in which the author would present an entire poker hand (usually one that the author himself had once encountered) and ask the reader what the correct play in that hand was. The author would then reveal what the actual correct play in the hand was, and the reasoning behind it. Here is an example of a practice hand from Bob Ciaffone's book *Middle Limit Holdem* (the first poker book I ever read, by the way):

A $30-$60 game. You are in the big blind holding A♣ -J♠. An early player, a middle player, the button, and the small blind limp [call the blind]. There is $150 in the pot and five players. The flop comes: A♦-9♣-8♣, giving you top pair, fair kicker and a backdoor nut flush-draw [three cards to the highest possible flush]. The small blind checks. You bet. The early player folds. The middle player raises. The button reraises. The small blind folds. What do you do?

Answer: Fold. Your one pair must fold when raised and re-raised. Someone almost certainly has two pair and maybe more. When you are beat, you are either dead to two perfect cards or playing three outs. If by some miracle you are ahead, you will frequently get overtaken on the turn or at the river. It could even get raised again. You do not have enough hand to be taking multi-bet rides on every street.

Each book devoted a considerable number of its pages to these practice hands. Ciaffone's book alone contained over four hundred of them (in fact, it was little *but* practice hands). And it was from these (and those in other books) that I derived the categorical rules that would then orchestrate my postflop play during a game.

Now, these practice hands were different from the direct categorical mandates for preflop play that told me exactly what action to take under each set of circumstances. But in order to apply this information to my actual play, I found it absolutely necessary to mold each book's advice into a strict set of categorical rules that would tell me exactly which action was the correct one in which situation. I simply *needed* the same kind of categorical guidelines that I had for preflop situations to orchestrate my play for *every* part of the game. And I could not conceive, at least at the time, of any other way to make my decisions.

Still, it is easy to see how I could transform these practice hands into categorical rules. Each practice hand would essentially serve as a prototype for a rule, which basically said: "In hands very similar to this one, do this." I also looked for *patterns* among the mass of practice hands the authors presented me with, and would distil from them more *general* rules that I could then apply in a much broader range of situations. I did this by finding multiple hands that, although they had substantial differences, all had the same correct play (at least according to the author). I would then attempt to consolidate the similarities between these hands into the basis of a wider categorical rule, and would draw the boundaries for this rule (that is, determine the situations in which it did not apply) by using practice hands that were sufficiently similar, but in which the correct play was different.

Of course the authors were more than obliging in this. In fact, it was their explicit intention to "impart the general principles of play and use concrete examples [that is, practice hands] to illustrate those principles being put to work," as Ciaffone so eloquently stated in *Middle Limit Holdem*. Here is an example of this kind of "general principle:"

Proper play on the turn generally calls for aggressiveness. . . People will call on the flop, especially in a raised pot, on some really raggedy stuff . . . and often release their dish-rag when the limit doubles [on the turn]—if you bet again. . . . You may be the preflop raiser with hands such as A-K or A-Q and fail to buy help on the flop. But because there are only one or two opponents, you attempt to purchase the pot with a flop bet. If someone calls and an innocent card comes on the turn, it is usually right to fire again and hope the double-size bet induces a fold.

Now, here is this principle being illustrated in practice hands:

A $15-$30 game. You raise from early position holding the A♥-K♦ after another early player limps. Only a middle player and the early limper call. There is $115 in the pot and three players. The flop is: 9♥-4♠-2♦, leaving you with only overcards. The early limper checks. You bet, and only the middle player calls. There is $145 in the pot and two players. The turn is the T♥. What do you do?

Answer: Bet. If you check, then you must fold if your opponent bets. . . . [But] by betting now, the opponent may fold, since players often bail out on the expensive street if they have anything less than top pair or an overpair.

A $15-$30 game. You are on the button holding the A♥-K♥. The cutoff [the player directly to the right of the button] opens with a raise and you reraise. Only the cutoff calls. There is $115 in the pot and two players. The flop comes: J♠-8♦-7♣, leaving you with only overcards. Your opponent checks. You bet and he calls. There is $145 in the pot. The turn is the 2♣. He checks. What do you do?

Answer: Bet. It would be bad poker to check now. . . . When you check in these situations, here is what you are telling your opponent: "I don't have a thing. Feel free to step in on the next round with a bet and take the pot." . . . He does not know whether you have A-K or a big pair on the betting to this point. . . . And you may be able to win the pot outright.

There were several more similar examples where the correct answer was to bet. Then the author presented a hand that, by contradistinction, illustrated the limits of this principle.

A $30-$60 game. You are on the button holding the A♥-K♣. Everyone folds to the cutoff, who opens with a raise. You reraise and only the cutoff calls. There is $230 in the pot and two players. The flop is: 7♣-6♣-4♥, leaving you with two big overcards and a backdoor flush draw. Your opponent checks. You bet and he calls. There is $290 in the pot. The turn is a 5♠. Your opponent checks. What do you do?

Answer: Check. This is an exception to the rule about following through with a bet on the turn after showing all the strength before and on the flop. With an open-ended straight on the table, there are many hands where your opponent has you drawing dead. By betting, you are also exposed to a check-raise bluff or semi-bluff.

Of course, I readily seized on such things and made them into categorical rules to play by. And the categories I distilled from the above hands should be obvious. They were: 'In situations where I raised or reraised preflop with high cards, got called, missed the flop, made a continuation bet, and got called by only one opponent, the correct play is to make another continuation bet on the turn . . . *except* when the board was exceptionally dangerous, in which case the correct play is to check.'

Now it might appear that this is a perfectly natural method of assimilating information, and it may well have been the author's intention that the reader do precisely this; but I want to make absolutely clear the convoluted kind of cognitive process I employed in forming these categories. What I did was first accept as true the author's conclusions as to what the correct play in a practice hand was, and then I used those final judgments of the author as the primary basis, the raw material, from which to build my categorical rules. Notice that at no point in this process must reasoning ever come into play. All that is required are the characteristics of the hand (so it can be categorized), and the correct *answer* for how to play it, to lay down the categorical rule for that type of situation.

Now certainly the authors *did* provide reasons to support their conclusions about the correct play in a hand (for their preflop guidelines as well as their practice hands). And I cannot say I ignored those reasons completely—I didn't. But those reasons most certainly took a second seat to the conclusions, and I employed them primarily as a *justification* for a conclusion I already accepted, as opposed to assessing them critically. This was essentially the process of reasoning and rationality in reverse. Instead of reasoning first and then using the resulting reasons as a basis from which to form conclusions, I accepted the conclusions first, and only then found reasons to support them.

This reverse of the normal process of rationality, in which reasons normally lead to conclusions, is what psychologists call "rationalization"—where a conclusion is accepted first, and reasons are only added later, *ad hoc*. Notice that in this process of rationalization, once a person accepts a conclusion as true, the actual reasons he then uses to support it are of little consequence. Since the purpose of this rationalized reasoning is to lead up to a predetermined conclusion, any chain of reasoning that *does not* lead to that conclusion must be dismissed (no matter how valid) and only one that does lead to it (no matter how faulty, shallow, or superficial it is) can be accepted. The result of this process is that reasons are often contorted, tailored to the conclusions, and become, in the end, essentially decorative.

It was in this backward manner that I learned to play poker from these books. And the reason I took this approach is clear. It is that I trusted an author's authority—his claim to knowledge and expertise—over my own reasoning and judgment. After all, each of these authors was an extremely successful professional poker player and had made great sums of money playing the game, while I was a complete novice and knew little to nothing about the right way to play poker. And that was, of course, why I turned to the books in the first place: to *learn* the right way to play poker, and to become a winning player myself. So if my own rationale for how to play a hand ever led to a different conclusion from that of an author's, I would invariably accept his judgment over my own—even if I didn't exactly *understand* the logic behind it.

I had no cause to doubt that the authors' judgment was correct—their success and their massive winnings in the game spoke sufficiently to that. And while I at times didn't fully understand the reasons they gave for playing a hand in a certain way, that didn't make that play any less *right*. It was simple: They knew how to play and I didn't. And I would do just as well making the same plays they did in the same situations, whether I understood the reasons for doing so or not.

Now, as for the reasons themselves, which the authors gave for the plays they recommended, these too (as you may have guessed) had their faults. In fact, they had a few very specific faults, to understand which requires that we go in greater detail into the mechanics of the game of poker.

DAVID SKLANSKY, EXPECTATION, AND THE MATHEMATICS OF POKER

Now, it is true that when I first began playing poker seriously — shortly after reading *Middle Limit Holdem* — I played almost exclusively by emulating the correct plays that were handed to me in book form, while understanding little to nothing about why I should make them. I obtained all the categorical rules I played by in the exact manner described above, and each rule existed in the form of a strict edict to fold, call, or raise in a specific type of situation. It is certainly worth noting, however, that even this dogmatic approach to decision making made me a consistent winner in the games between friends at school and in the small-stakes games online.

But as I played more and more poker and read many additional poker books, my understanding of the game grew. Specifically, the books of one poker author, David Sklansky, had the greatest effect in shaping my understanding of the game. Sklansky was, and undoubtedly still is, the name in instructional poker books. The entire serious poker community reads and plays by his books. And there really is no better teacher of the game, at least the mathematical part of it, than he. He has written fourteen books on gambling so far — nine of them on poker in particular. And of the more than a dozen poker books I read before the third volume of *Harrington on Hold'em*, Sklansky was the author or co-author of about half.

His books tremendously advanced my understanding of poker. They taught me the fundamental principles of probability and mathematics that underlie every aspect of the game, and lucidly explained how these principles directly determined the correct play in virtually all poker situations. I was quite proficient at mathematics from a very early age, and was always one of the top math students in my class. So I readily grasped the mathematical concepts that these books presented. As a result, I now not only knew the correct plays to make in most poker situations, but thoroughly understood the reasons why they were correct as well—at least on a strictly mathematical basis.

Yet despite this development, I was still a long way from mastering the game. And this was because math is only one half of poker. The other half is *judgment*. And while Sklansky perfectly understood the mathematical part of poker and accurately explained even its most subtle nuances; he had only a partial understanding of the judgment part of the game, and his explanations of it were vague and incomplete. The reader will understand what I mean shortly. For now, I want to expound in greater detail on the mathematical concepts I learned from Sklansky's books and the way this affected my decision-making process in the game.

The most important thing Sklansky's books taught me is this: Every poker decision is essentially a unique gambling proposition. And just like for any other gamble, the correct decision in a poker hand is determined by (1) the amount of money you stand to win, (2) the amount you have to risk to win it, and (3) the percent chance that you actually will win it. In poker, the amount you stand to win is usually the amount in the pot; or, more accurately, the amount that will be in the pot by the time the hand is over. The amount you have to risk is the additional amount you have to put into the pot, whether by betting or calling, in your efforts to win the hand. And your percent chance of winning is the overall probability that you will end up taking the pot, either by showing down the best hand or by having all your opponents fold before the showdown.

The mathematical principle that determines the correct play in a poker hand is the same one that determines whether any gambling proposition is profitable or not: The principle of *expectation*. A gamble's expectation is the overall monetary amount you can expect to win or lose *on average* if you accept that gamble. The expectation of a gamble is easy to calculate: Your expectation is the amount of money you stand to win, multiplied by your percent chance of winning the gamble; minus the amount of money you have to risk, multiplied by your percent chance of losing the gamble.

Gamblers usually refer to a number called their *odds* to make these calculations. A gamble's odds is simply the ratio between the amount of money the gamble pays if you win and the amount you have to pay if you lose.

For example: If you roll a fair six-sided die, and a friend agrees to pay you $6 if you roll a six, and you agree to pay him $1 if you roll any number one through five, your odds are $6-to-$1. Your expectation for this gamble is therefore ($6 * 1/6) – ($1 * 5/6); a sixth of a dollar, or about eighteen cents. This means that, for each roll, you can expect to win eighteen cents from your friend (on average). Because your expectation here is positive, it is correct to take this gamble.[12] If you roll the die six times, you can expect your friend to owe you one dollar. If you roll the die six hundred times, you can expect your friend to owe you one hundred dollars. And so forth. It is on this principle that professional poker players and professional gamblers in general make their living.

To quote David Sklansky: "To win at poker you must make as many plays with a positive expectation as possible, while avoiding those with a negative one. You have three choices each time you act during a poker hand: fold, call, and raise* ["Betting is just raising when the current bet is zero. Likewise, checking is just calling when the current bet is zero"]. Each of these plays has an expectation associated with it. *Your goal is simply to choose the one with the highest expectation.*" For instance: If there is $80 in the pot and you have to call $20 to win it, if your chance to win is greater than 20%, you should call; if it is less than 20%, you should fold; and if your chance to win is so

---

[12] Notice that the reason you can expect to profit here, and not simply break even, is that in a gamble you don't have to pay your opponent if you win. If you structured the wager so that you had to pay your friend $1 merely to roll the die, and he would then pay you $6 if you won, that would result in an expectation of zero. But because you don't pay him when you roll a six, this is a better than even-money wager.

great that you are willing to risk even more money to win more from your opponent, you should raise. All decision making in poker essentially boils down to this kind of calculation.

Here are some examples of how this applies in an actual poker hand:

There are three players in a $10-$20 Limit Hold'em game: (1) The big blind, who is in for $10, (2) The small blind, who is in for $5, and (3) The button, who is in for nothing and is first to act preflop. The player on the button has A♠K♠, the player in the small blind has 4♠4♦, and the player in the big blind has Q♠5♠. Now, if all the players stay in the pot to the river, the ace-king has a 42.5% chance of ending up with the best hand once all five board cards are dealt, the pocket fours has a 33.1% chance, and the queen-five has a 24.4% chance.[13] To simplify matters, let us discount any betting that can be expected on the future rounds and focus only on the *preflop* expectation of these players.[14]

The ace-king, since he is a substantial favorite in this pot, is certainly not going to fold his hand. In fact, since he has a definite edge here over his opponents (his 42.5% being greater than the one-in-three chance he would need to break even), it is clearly in his best interest to raise and exploit this edge. Notice that if he simply calls the $10, the small blind will call the additional $5, and the big blind will check. There will be $30 in the pot, and the ace-king will have put in $10 to win $20. His expectation in that case would be a positive $2.75.[15] If he

---

[13] There is a 0.54% chance of a three-way tie, which is accounted for as an additional .18% (0.54% divided by three) probability of winning for each player.

[14] In actual play, the expected action on future rounds *does* have to be taken into account when calculating the expectation of a hand. And this adds a further layer of complexity to the game (but more about this later). For the sake of our current example, let us just assume that once the preflop round is over, none of the players will make any more bets on the postflop rounds—simply letting the five cards be dealt on the board, and showing down their hands on the river, with whomever ends up having the best hand winning the pot.

[15] ($20 * 42.5%) − ($10 * 57.5%) = $2.75

raises to $20, however, both the blinds will call, and he will now have put $20 into the pot to win $40. His expectation in this case will be exactly twice that of merely calling, for a total of $5.50. Poker players call this kind of raise, to get more money into the pot when you are a favorite, a raise "for value."

Notice that the more money a player can get into a pot when he is a favorite, the higher his expectation will be. If one of the other players in the above example decides to reraise (for some reason) and makes everyone put $30 into the pot, the ace-king's expectation will now grow even higher, to a total of $8.25. And, of course, if someone else *does* reraise, the ace-king should put in yet another (third) raise for value, making all the players put $40 into the pot, and increasing his expectation to the highest possible $11. (Four bets is usually the maximum allowed on a single round of betting in a standard poker game.)

Now let's look at this situation from another player's perspective. The big blind has only a 24.4% chance of winning the pot with his queen-five. He is clearly not a favorite. However, when the button raises and the small blind calls, it only costs him $10 more to call in a $50 pot. He is getting $50-to-$10 odds with a 24.4% chance of winning, which amounts to a positive expectation of $4.64. This ratio between the amount in the pot and the amount a player has to call on the current round is what poker players call the "pot odds."[16] Since the queen-five has a positive expectation for calling, he should call this raise. Poker players call this a straightforward "odds play," and it is one of the most fundamental plays in the game. (It need not be said that raising would be incorrect for this player and would have a much lower expectation than just calling.)

Finally, let us look at the situation from the small blind's perspective. He is certainly not going to fold when the button raises, since it costs him only $15 more to call in what will be a $60 pot with a 33.1%

---

[16] This is as opposed to the "expected odds," or the "implied odds," which takes into account the money that will go into the pot on the future rounds, as well as the additional amount a player will have to risk on those future rounds (which I will discuss later).

chance of winning. Those are $45-to-$15 pot odds, and thus a positive expectation of $4.86 for calling.[17] Also, since he is not a favorite with his pocket fours (his 33.1% chance to win being lower than 33.33%), his hand isn't strong enough to raise for value. Yet, let us see what happens if he raises anyway. The button raised to $20, and he now reraises to $30, which has the very important effect of putting the big blind in a bad position. Now, the big blind will have no choice but to fold his queen-five. From the big blind's perspective again, instead of the $10 he would have to call initially if the small blind didn't reraise, he now has to call $20, *plus* another $10 more when the button inevitably caps it to four bets with his ace-king. He would therefore have to call $30 to win $90,[18] which would give him a negative expectation of minus $0.72 for calling. Since folding always has an expectation of exactly $0, it is the better play now over calling. And now look what happens to the small blind's expectation.

With the big blind out, there are now only two players in the pot, and the pocket fours' chances of winning actually rise from his original 33.1%, against the two opponents, to a whopping 51.6% against the ace-king alone. He actually becomes the *favorite* in the hand. The ace-king's chances of winning also rise, but only to 48.4%. And since he now has a less than 50% chance of winning the pot with only two players, he is no longer the favorite and cannot put in the fourth raise for value with his ace-king. He will therefore only call the small blind's reraise, and the pocket fours, who has now put $25 more into the pot to win $45,[19] will have a resulting expectation of $11.12. This is a huge deal higher than his original expectation of $4.86 had he only called! The play that the small blind made here is what poker players call raising "to protect your hand." Unlike a raise for value, it is a raise designed to increase your chances of winning the pot (and thereby your expectation) by eliminating players who can't profitably call that

---

[17] ($45 * 33.1%) – ($15 * 66.9) = $4.86

[18] $40 from the button, $40 from the small blind, and the $10 originally posted by the big blind

[19] The $30 from the button, the $10 from the big blind, and the $5 small blind he himself initially posted

raise. From these examples, we can see what a profound effect the mathematical principle of expectation has on poker decisions and strategy.

One final thing I want to point out here, which might have been a source of confusion for some readers, is how it can be possible, in some cases, for all of the players involved in a hand to have a positive expectation. After all, as David Sklansky so correctly pointed out: "Money does not appear from nowhere or disappear into nowhere: *If one person has a positive expectation, another must have a negative one, and the sum of all expectations must be zero.*" Well, the answer is: Because of the blinds. There is $15 in the pot posted by the big and small blinds before the hand even begins. That is what starts the game. The players in the hand are essentially competing for that initial "dead money" already in the pot. As David Sklansky puts it: "All poker starts as a struggle for the [blinds]."

A GAME OF INCOMPLETE INFORMATION, READING HANDS, AND THE ART OF POKER

Now, as we saw in the above examples, each hand has a precise and calculable winning percentage against every other hand or group of hands. These probabilities are simply the chances that a hand will end up as the best hand on the river once all the cards have been dealt. Of course, these percentages change every time a new card is dealt on the board; but on every single betting round, this probability can be precisely and mathematically calculated for every hand. These probabilities are fairly easy to calculate postflop (when there are at most two new cards to come), but even for the preflop probabilities there are now plenty of computer programs that can calculate these to a hundredth of a percent.[20]

To quote David Sklansky: "If everybody's cards were showing at all times, there would be a precise and mathematically correct play for

---

[20] That is what I used to get the winning percentages for each hand in previous example.

each player. Any player who deviated from his correct play would be reducing his mathematical expectation and increasing the expectation of his opponents." "Of course," Sklansky added, "if all cards were exposed at all times, there wouldn't be a game of poker."

Indeed, the entire basis and challenge of poker is that you cannot see your opponent's cards. As Sklansky stated in his extraordinarily insightful book, *The Theory of Poker:* "Poker, like all card games, is a game of incomplete information." And as he elucidated in a different book: "There are two important pieces of information you do not have: (1) Your opponents' cards (2) How your opponents will respond to your action."

This means that, in your attempts to calculate your expectation in a hand, you cannot exactly determine the amount of money you have to risk in it, because you don't know whether or not your opponents will raise and make the hand more expensive for you. You also cannot determine the exact amount of money you stand to win in a hand, because you don't know whether or not your opponents will actually call and pay you off with their weaker hands. And most importantly, you cannot exactly calculate your chances of winning a hand, because you don't know what hand or hands you are actually up against.

The effect of this for trying to determine your odds in a hand, is that you cannot simply go by your pot odds on the present round (which you always know) but must try and determine what Sklansky called your "effective odds" for the hand as a whole, by taking into account the betting action on future rounds.

To quote Sklansky's *Theory of Poker*:

When you compute odds on a hand you intend to play to the end, you must think not in terms of the immediate pot odds but in terms of the total amount you might lose versus the total amount you might win. You have to ask, "What do I lose if I miss my hand, and what do I gain if I make it?" The answer to this question tells you your *real* or *effective* odds.

This, however, is by far the easier part of filling in the incomplete pieces of information in a poker hand. "Figuring effective odds may sound complicated," Sklansky wrote in *The Theory of Poker*, "but it is a simple matter of addition:"

> You add all the calls you will have to make, assuming you play to the end, to determine the total amount you will lose if you don't make [the best] hand. Then compare this figure to the total amount you should win if you do make [the best] hand. This total is the money in the pot at the moment plus all the future bets you can expect to win, excluding your own future bets. Thus, if there is $100 in the pot at the moment and three more $20 betting rounds, you are getting $160-to-$60 effective odds if both you and your opponent figure to call all bets. If you know you won't call on the end unless you make your hand, your effective odds become $160-to-$40. When you think your opponent won't call on the end if your card hits, your effective odds would be reduced to something like $140-to-$40. If, on early betting rounds, these odds are greater than your chances of making [the best] hand, you are correct to see the hand through to the end. If they are not, you should fold.

Of course, calculating these effective odds requires a good amount of *predicting* how your opponents are going to act. What requires a much greater amount of predicating, however, is what hand your opponent or opponents actually have. To quote Sklansky again: "If you have ace-king, your expectation when your opponent has pocket queens is radically different from when he has pocket aces. You could ask him to show you his cards to aid your calculations, but he would probably not oblige. Thus, most calculations of expectation in poker must be *estimates*, based on logical guesses at your opponents' hands."

This is the judgment part of poker. And it is of course precisely this aspect of *judgment* that makes poker a true game of skill, rather than rote mathematical calculation. "The art of poker," Sklansky wrote, "is filling the gaps in the incomplete information provided by your opponent's betting."[21] This *art* of discerning an opponent's hand, and predicting how he is going to play it from the plays he made *earlier* in the hand, is the process Sklansky called "reading hands." And it is his skill in reading hands that accounts for the bulk of an expert player's profits from playing the game.

After all, an expert poker player's *long-term* expectation depends not only on how well he plays his hands, but also on how well his opponents play theirs. To quote Sklansky: "If your opponents all played 'perfect' poker, you could not possibly win in the long run. On nights when your cards ran much better than average, you would win. When your cards ran worse than average, you would lose. Overall, though, no matter how well you played, you could not beat the game long-term."

This is because, by the fundamental principles of probability and because the cards in a poker game are dealt at random, each player can expect, in the long run, to find himself in the exact same situation with the exact same hand just as frequently as any other player. So even if a player plays perfect poker and makes the optimal plays in every single hand, he can only expect to break even if all of his opponents *also* play perfect poker and make those same plays against him when they find themselves in the same situations. To quote Sklansky's *Theory of Poker:*

> Your edge comes not from holding better cards [than your opponents], but from play in situations where your opponents would play incorrectly if they had your hand and you had theirs. The total amount of money they cost themselves in incorrect play, assuming you play perfectly, minus the rake, is the amount of money you will win. Your opponents' various

---

[21] There is a second part to this quote. "The art of poker," writes Sklansky, is (1) "filling the gaps in the incomplete information provided by your opponent's betting," while (2) "at the same time preventing your opponents from discovering any more than what you want them to know about your hand." This second part, however, pales in importance compared to the first; and I will explain it in detail further in the book.

mistakes . . . cost them various amounts of money. If the hands were reversed, you wouldn't make these mistakes, and this difference is your [profit].

Therefore, if your opponents could see your hands and you could see theirs, the only thing that would give a player any advantage over another is being a better mathematician. Both players would have every bit of information they need to calculate their expectations down to the penny. If one player consistently made mistakes in his calculations or didn't know how to apply the principle of expectation, he would lose to the player who understood expectation and made no such mistakes. Of course, most even semi-competent poker players *do* understand expectation (in fact, probably because they have read Sklansky's books), and making the required mathematical calculations becomes extremely easy for almost anyone with practice.

In fact, in the course of an actual poker game between relatively competent players, the expert players really do make the lion's share of their profits not because they are better at calculating expectation than their opponents, but because they are better able to determine what cards their opponents hold, and to anticipate the plays they are going to make before they make them. They do this by *reading hands.*

As Sklansky writes, "In hold'em, any time an opponent bets, calls, or raises, good players ask, 'What could my opponent have done that with?'" *This is the basis of reading hands.* "You analyze the meaning of an opponent's check, bet, or raise, and you look at the exposed cards [on the board] and try to judge from them what his . . . hand might be." This is done by "put[ting] these two pieces of evidence together — the plays [an opponent made] and the cards on the board — to draw a conclusion about an opponent's most likely hand." "In other words," Sklansky writes, "you use logic to read hands."

But other than the specific information you have in a hand from your opponent's betting and the cards on the board, hand reading also involves utilizing the more general information you have about each opponent and his personal playing tendencies. "Reading hands is both an art and a science," Sklansky writes:

> It is an art because you must know your opponents. Before you can technically analyze what your opponents might have, you must have played with them for a considerable length of time, seen how they play their hands against you, and most importantly, watched them play hands in which you are not involved. . . . You want to discover how your opponents tend to play the various hands they might have. Will a particular opponent raise with strong hands in early position, or will he slowplay? Will he raise on a draw? How does he play his big hands from one round of betting to the next? How often does he bluff? The more you know about an opponent's general playing habits, the less difficulty you will have reading what he might be holding in a specific situation.

For example: If I observed that an opponent would usually check-raise in a certain situation when he had a legitimately strong hand but bet out directly when he was bluffing, I could assume that a check-raise from him in that situation likely meant strength and was unlikely to be a bluff, while a bet meant weakness and was very possibly a bluff. This is what poker players call having a "read" on an opponent.[22]

Of course, it is rarely possible, except in the most favorable cases, to determine the *exact* hand an opponent holds through hand reading. Instead, the best you can usually do in trying to read your opponent's hand is, as Sklansky put it, "1.) Determine the possible hands your opponent may have, [and] 2.) Assess the chances of his having each of his possible hands." For example: Given the opponent I'm playing against, his betting throughout the hand, and the cards on the board,

---

[22] It's also possible to use an opponent's physical *tells* to read his hand; but Sklansky's books were concerned mostly with the *mathematics* of the game, and he almost entirely ignored this aspect. And since I primarily played online and wasn't very good at reading physical tells when playing in person, I also completely ignored this aspect.

I can tell in this situation that he either has *Hand A, Hand B,* or *Hand C,* and that there is a 45% chance he has *Hand A,* a 30% chance he has *Hand B,* and a 25% chance he has *Hand C.*

It is therefore these sets of possible hands and the opponent's probability of having them that must then be used to calculate your expectation. This is done by calculating the expectation a play has against *each* of the possible hands the opponent can hold, then multiplying those expectations by the respective probabilities of him actually having each of those hands, and finally adding the resulting values together to get your total average expectation for the play. For instance, here is a situation that occasionally comes up in No Limit Hold'em:

You raise preflop with ace-king suited, and a solid opponent who you know would only reraise you with A-A or K-K reraises you all in. He of course has an equal chance of having either hand, and the all-in means that there can be no further betting on later rounds. The pot is now offering you $400-to-$100 odds to call this bet. Now, against the A-A your hand has only a 12.14% chance of winning.[23] If your opponent had that hand, your expectation for calling would be negative $39.30 and you would clearly be correct to fold. Against the K-K, however, your hand has a much more robust 34.1% chance of winning, which makes the expectation for calling a *positive* $70.50, and therefore the correct play if he has K-K. Now, since the opponent has a 50% chance of having A-A and a 50% chance of having K-K, to get your total expectation for calling in this situation you must multiply your *minus* $39.30 expectation against Ace-Ace by 50% and your *plus* $70.50 expectation against King-King by 50% and add them together to get your total expectation of $15.60 for calling this bet. Since this expectation is positive, you should call.[24]

---

[23] This includes half of the 1.26% chance of getting a draw and winning only half the pot.

[24] Notice, however, that if you were getting only $300-to-$100 odds on your call, your expectation for calling against the A-A would be negative $51.44 and against K-K a positive $37.40. The average expectation would then be negative $7.02, and therefore folding would be the correct play.

Now, it is of course true that the opponent can only have one hand at any one time. And if you could see what that hand was, you would certainly be able to make better and more profitable decisions. But because the only way you can tell what your opponent has is by looking at his betting, the best you can do is calculate your average expectation against all his possible hands—as determined by hand reading— while adjusting for the probability of him holding each one.

Now, one more important thing about the process of hand reading is that it has to be performed differently depending on the opponent you are up against. Since a big part of the process is getting a *read* on an opponent, and because getting a read on an opponent requires long term observation, there really are three different types of opponents you can face, and thus three corresponding methods of reading hands that must be applied for each one.

In fact, the only opponent it's possible to get a true read on is a strategically inept and inexperienced one. This is the kind of player who doesn't have a good understanding of the game, and whose play is determined more by his own peculiar tendencies than by any considerations of proper poker strategy or the mathematical demands of his hand and the situation. The reads good players can have on such an opponent are really just their observations of his mistakes. And it is only against this kind of opponent that it is possible to tell that he can have *Hand A* in a certain situation but not *Hand B* because you have observed that he nearly always plays *Hand A* one way and *Hand B* another.

Against an experienced and mathematically savvy opponent, however, hand reading has to be performed on a different basis. Such a player will rarely make mistakes, and his play is guided not by his unique proclivities, but by sound mathematical analysis and a striving to make the correct play at every stage of a hand. The only thing you could really learn from observing such an opponent is that he *is* in fact a skilled and technically sound player. And to read this kind of opponent's hand requires looking at his betting not in the context of his peculiar playing tendencies, but in the context of the situation itself and the correct plays that it calls for.

Since there are many incorrect ways to play a hand, but only one correct way, the hand reading process can be applied uniformly against all seasoned and competent players.[25] First, you can assume that a player you know to be good will consistently recognize and make the correct play on every stage of a hand. Of course, what those correct plays are will depend on the hand that he actually holds. By that logic, you can conclude that if a skilled opponent makes a sequence of plays that would have been correct with *Hand A* but not with *Hand B*, then he may very possibly have *Hand A*, but is very unlikely to have *Hand B*.

In this way, you can read the hands of an experienced opponent. Notice, however, that although there may be only one correct play for any given hand, there can be and often are many different hands for which a certain play is correct. This is why hand reading cannot usually determine an opponent's *exact* hand. Instead, as Sklansky said, you "put an opponent on a variety of hands at the start of play, and as play progresses, eliminate some of those hands based on his later play and on the cards that appear on the board. Through this process of elimination, you should have a good idea of what the opponent has when the last card is dealt."

Finally, the third type of player you can be up against, and against who you have to employ a different method of hand reading, is the *unknown opponent*. This is an opponent who you have never seen before or have not observed long enough to obtain any read on. Thus, you simply do not know whether he is a solid player, a novice, or a complete maniac.

There is, however, a good way to read an unknown opponent's hand, and that is to assume that he is a solid player until proven otherwise. The idea behind this is that you can still expect to make a profit by playing against a bad player *as if* he was a good one, but not the

---

[25] To put it another way: All good players play (more or less) the same, while all bad players play differently.

other way around. This is because the bad player will simply make too many mistakes by playing poorly to make up for the mistakes you will make against him by giving his plays too much respect.[26] To quote Sklansky: "There is almost no question that if your opponent plays badly, and you continue to play *assuming* he plays well, you will still win." "But," he added, "you will not win as much as someone who is adjusting to his poor play."

This is what we may call the *conservative* approach to reading an unknown opponent. To remedy this, you can therefore play *as if* your opponent was a good player, but also incorporate a 10% probability in your calculations that he is an absolute maniac and will show down a hand that makes absolutely no sense. Such an approach may make your calculations a little more accurate until you obtain more information about your unknown opponent. But in any case, after several rounds of play, the true nature of an opponent will be quick to reveal itself to a careful observer.

Now, a final thing I left out about the "judgment" part of poker, but which the clever reader might have already figured out, is the way you can predict how an opponent will play on the future betting rounds of a hand (the second missing piece of information in a poker game). This is, in fact, merely a further extension of hand reading. Just as you can determine your opponent's possible hands from the plays he made and his personal playing tendencies, so can you predict the plays he is *going* to make from the hands he can have and his personal playing tendencies.

For example: If your hand reading tells you that your opponent has a 20% chance of having *Hand A*, a 30% chance of having *Hand B*, and a 50% chance of having *Hand C*, and you know that if you bet at him he will fold *Hand A*, call with *Hand B*, and raise with *Hand C*, then you can predict that when you bet, he will fold 20% of the time, call

---

[26] And, of course, if you do not give enough respect to the plays of a solid opponent, he simply will take your money.

30% of the time, and raise 50% of the time (with each of those respective hands).

It is important to understand, by the way, that even though an opponent can only have one hand at any one time, these probabilities are not simply arbitrary concepts. In a very real sense, if a player will make the exact same plays in the exact same situation with multiple different hands, and you have no information about his hand other than his betting, then there is a definite *objective* probability that he will have each of his possible hands in each unique situation.[27]

ESTIMATES FROM EXPERIENCE, STATISTICS, AND CATEGORICAL HAND READING

Now, up to this point, everything Sklansky wrote about hand reading was certainly good and true. But as I mentioned earlier, he was primarily a mathematician, and he had only a partial understanding of this *judgment* part of the game. Specifically, he was mistaken about two major aspects of hand reading. His first mistake was that, in the way he conceived of hand reading in his books (and in all likelihood the way he performed it in practice as well), he reasoned *exclusively* in terms of categories of hands. And this led directly to his second mistake, which was assuming that the only way for a player to determine what the probability was that the opponent had each of these categories of hands, was by experience.

Here is an example of this kind of categorical hand reading as Sklansky describes it in *The Theory of Poker*. In this example the game is $10-$20 Limit Hold'em, the pot is small (under $60 Sklansky says), your hand is K♠Q♠, you are second to act against a single opponent, and the board is K♦9♥6♠-2♣ on the turn.

Sklansky sets up the preceding action: "Your opponent, who is a good player, checked and called your bet on the flop. When the deuce

---

[27] We'll have an opportunity to look at this in greater detail later in the book.

falls [on the turn], your opponent checks again." The decision you have to make, then, is: "Should you check or bet your pair of kings?"

To begin your hand reading, Sklansky says, you have to "think of the various hands the opponent might have to do what he did. So when your opponent called your bet on the flop and then checked on [the turn], you [must] try to determine what hands he might have that prompted him to play the way he did."

Now here is Sklanksy's categorical analysis of the situation: "Your opponent could be slowplaying a better hand than yours—say, K-9 or 6-6. You estimate there's a 25 percent chance he has such a hand. He might have a fairly good hand such as K-J or K-T. You figure those hands at 25 percent, too. Your opponent might have a mediocre hand like K-4 or A-9 or 10-10. The chances of those hands you put at 35 percent. And you figure there's a 15 percent chance your opponent has 87 and is drawing to a straight."

Sklansky sums this up in a diagram:

Opponent's Possible Hands	Approximate Chances
Better [hand] than Yours	25 percent
Mediocre hand	35 percent
Fair hand (K-J or K-T)	25 percent
Straight draw	15 percent

Finally, Sklansky predicts from this the opponent's future actions: "You know that if you bet on [the turn] after his check, your opponent will probably call with his fair hands, with a straight draw, and at least call with his big hands. However this player will probably fold his mediocre hands because the pot is not big enough to justify calling with them." After taking all this into consideration, Sklansky decides on the correct play in this hand: "Therefore, after your opponent checks on [the turn], it turns out the correct play may be to check it right back. Your intentions are to bet on the [river] if your opponent checks and call if he bets." "Because you expect your opponent to fold his mediocre hands if you bet on [the turn], and you want to win at least one more bet from those hands, the correct play 60 percent of the time is to check. It is correct to bet only 40 percent of the time. . . . Therefore, you check."

Now, this all seems reasonable. And it may indeed be difficult to see with the untrained eye what the issue here might be. Notice, however, that Sklansky's *Hand A, Hand B, Hand C,* and *Hand D* in this analysis are not *individual hands* like Ace-Ace, King-Jack, Six-Six, or Ten-Nine, but *categories of hands,* specifically "a better hand that yours", "a fairly good hand," "a mediocre hand," and "a straight draw." And the percentages he assigns are also not to any individual hands, but to these categories.

But this begs the question: By what means can we determine what the percentages for these categories are? And precisely there lies the problem. The fact is that if you reason exclusively in terms of categories of hands, the only way for you to determine the probability that the opponent actually has any of these categories is by intuitive estimates from experience. Sklansky describes this approach best in the following quote from *The Theory of Poker,* about making precisely this kind of estimate on the river:

> When all the cards are out, you must decide . . . [what] your chances [are] of having the best hand. It is a judgment problem more than a math problem because there is no way to calculate your chances of winning precisely. If you can beat only a bluff, you have to evaluate the chances that your opponent is bluffing. When you have a decent hand, you must evaluate the chances that your opponent is betting a worse hand than yours. Making these evaluations is often not easy. . . . Your ability to do so depends upon your experience, especially your ability to read hands and players. Some things can be learned only through trials of fire at the poker table.

The idea behind these kinds of estimates-from-experience is that you can use *statistics* to read hands. That is, rather than thinking 'How would this specific opponent play his hand?' you think 'How have I seen other players who are similar to this one play their hands?' This cannot be applied too successfully for reading *bad* players, since every bad player is unique and has his own specific proclivities. It can, however, be applied to good players, who all play more or less the same way (that is, correctly). And it can even be applied to unknown players, whose skill level you do not know, yet who—by the very fact that they sat down at the game you are currently playing in—can be considered a typical player at the current limit (at least until any further information about that player emerges).

It is done in the following manner. First, you look at your opponent's betting in the current hand and the cards on the board. Then, you have to draw on your experience from the thousands or tens of thousands of hands you have played against the hundreds of different opponents similar to this one over the course of your poker career. If you know your opponent to be a good player, you refer to your experience playing against good players. If he is an unknown player, you refer to your experience playing against *all* the players you have encountered at the current limit.[28] Finally, you make a *historical* assessment of what hands those opponents have held, and with what frequencies, when they made the same plays in the same situation as the current one.

For example: Because I had seen various opponents make the same sequence of plays in a certain situation dozens of times before, I could tell *from experience* that a similar opponent making those plays in that same situation will—on average—have top pair 20% of the time, middle pair 30% of the time, a draw 40% of the time, and a pure bluff 10% of the time. And so on.

This, of course, requires a lot of experience to do well—but it is actually quite practicable. After playing poker for several years, I became

---

[28] It is worth noting, by the way, that the average style and competence of play of your opponents *does* change from limit to limit. That is, players in a $5-$10 Hold'em game will play differently (usually worse) than players in a $10-$20 Hold'em game, who will play differently (worse) than players at a $20-$40 Hold'em game, and so on.

quite good at it myself. There is, nevertheless, a huge caveat to this approach. And it's that although an experienced player can make a pretty good ballpark estimate of these probabilities, he can rarely be very precise. As any science professor can tell you, and as the Nobel Prize winner Daniel Kahneman adroitly demonstrated in multiple psychological experiments: *Human beings are poor intuitive statisticians.*[29]

Professional poker players are no exception to this—something I can certainly attest to from my own experience. And Sklansky too admits this problem quite explicitly in the following description of hand reading:

> Hand reading is also an exercise in juggling probabilities. . . . Usually, the best you'll be able to do is to sort candidate holdings into categories like, 'Likely,' 'Somewhat likely,' or 'Unlikely.' You might observe the way a pot has played out and conclude, "She's probably either got a terrific hand, or she's bluffing, [and] it's unlikely that she's got a fairly good or [a] so-so hand."

The effect is clear: Once you choose to reason exclusively in terms of categories, even your math must become categorical.

I must, however, absolutely stress the word "exclusively" here. There is, in fact, nothing inherently wrong with this kind of categorical reasoning. In a lot of ways, it is actually extremely useful and sometimes completely indispensable. As I mentioned earlier in the categories section of this chapter, thinking in terms of categories of hands has several major benefits.[30] The true problem arises not merely

---

[29] As Kahneman so cleverly put it, after the results of a survey revealed that "even sophisticated statistical researchers," "including the authors of two statistical textbooks," consistently made inaccurate judgments of probability: "Even statisticians were not good intuitive statisticians." (*Thinking, Fast and Slow*, Kahneman, page 3)

[30] (1) The first is that it allows you to reduce the dozens of individual hands your opponent can hold to only a few general categories. (2) The second is that all the individual hands within a category will usually have

from thinking in terms of these categories, but from thinking exclusively in terms of these categories, without ever breaking them down into their individual hand constituents. The difficulty this creates, of course, is that it leaves no objective, mathematical way to determine the probability of the opponent actually having each of these categories of hands.

Yet this isn't a problem unique to Sklansky and his approach to the game. Every single other poker author I read (other than Dan Harrington) reasoned exclusively in terms of categories of hands. Many even reasoned in vague, categorical terms about the mathematical aspect of the game. Sklansky was simply the most explicit of them; meticulously analyzing the mathematics of the game, while resigning the parts of the game that required judgment to imprecise, categorical hand reading.

DECEPTION, GAME THEORY, AND READING YOUR OWN HANDS

The effect Sklansky's books had on my approach to and understanding of the game, therefore, was a peculiar one. Like Sklansky, I now understood the mathematical portion of the game extremely well. And also like Sklansky, my reasoning in the hand reading part of the game remained categorical. Thus, at this point in my poker development, the game was divided for me into two distinct parts: (1) The mathematical part, which required strict mathematical logic and precise calculation, and (2) The judgment part, which required the much more tenuous logic of hand reading and approximations based on experience.

---

about the same percent chance of winning against your hand—thus making it fairly easy to calculate your expectation against each of these categories of hands, without giving up much in the way of accuracy. (3) A third benefit we can now add is that you can usually expect an opponent to play all of the hands within a category more or less the same way, which of course also elegantly facilitates the process of hand reading.

I was, of course, fully comfortable with the mathematical part of the game, and was fully able to independently perform all of the calculations required in any given poker hand. It was the judgment part of the game that still gave me trouble, especially in those situations against good or unknown opponents that required employing my "experience." As usual, I often didn't trust my own judgments from experience. And to make up for it, I still frequently played by a set of strict categorical rules, which I obtained from one of the poker books or another in the exact manner I described earlier,[31] to absolve myself from having to make these kinds of judgments.

And all this was further complicated by the fact that hand reading is really a two-way street. That is, just as you base your decisions on what you read your opponents to have, your opponents (if they are any good) base their decisions on what they read you to have. And in the same way your expectation increases (at your opponent's expense) the better you're able to narrow down his holdings, your opponent's expectation increases (at your expense) the better he's able to narrow down yours.

For instance: If you could tell that you definitely had your opponent beat, you could push your hand harder and win more bets from him than if you were unsure. And if you could tell that your opponent definitely had you beat, you could simply fold your hand and save the bets you otherwise would have called off. You also could, of course, snap off your opponent's bluffs if you knew he was betting with nothing; and you could take advantage of good bluffing opportunities, if you knew he was likely to fold if you bet.[32] All this, of course, applies in reverse as well.

It is therefore a vital part of correct strategy (when you are up against players competent enough to read hands) to regularly employ "deception" to disguise your hands and thereby make them harder to

---

[31] See the "Rationalization" section.

[32] This is also the reason that having a "read" on your inexperienced opponents is so valuable. You simply make more money off of them when their bets reveal too much information about their hands. *In poker, information translates directly into profit.*

read. One poker book put it well: "Basically, there are only two kinds of deception. . . . You can act weaker than you really are by checking, failing to raise, or failing to reraise; [and] you can act stronger than you really are by betting, raising, or reraising without the normal requisite values for that action." The fundamental idea behind this is to deliberately make the same plays in the same situations with a variety of different hands, both strong and weak. So if in a certain spot you would frequently bet your good hands for value, you should occasionally bet your bad hands in the same situation as a bluff in order to disguise your hands. And if you frequently check-call or check-fold in a certain situation with your bad hands, you should occasionally check-call or check-raise with your good hands as a way to keep your opponents guessing. Of course, your better opponents will likely be using all the same tactics (correctly) against you. To quote Sklansky:

> As your opponents get tougher and tougher, your ability to read hands starts to fall off because tough players disguise their hands and they are sometimes intentionally inconsistent. They make tricky, ambiguous plays like semi-bluffing, like raising with the second-best hand, like slowplaying right to the end and then check-raising you. . . . They are trying as hard to deceive you about what they have as you are trying to discover what they have. And of course, you are presumably playing your hands equally hard against them, even as you are trying to read their hands.

And this adds another layer of complexity to poker, particularly the *judgment* part of it. The fact is, that because your expectation in a hand depends (partially) on your opponent's future actions, and your opponent's future actions depend on how much the plays you make tell him about your hand, you have to take special care that your plays are not revealing too much information (to your observant opponents) about the cards you are holding. In other words, you have to make sure your opponents don't get a read on you.

For example: If in the same situation you check-raise when you have a good hand but simply bet out when you decide to bluff, an observant opponent will quickly catch on that a check-raise means you are strong and a bet means you are weak. Taken separately, therefore, each of these plays may very well seem like the most profitable alternative: Check-raising with a good hand wins two bets from your opponent when successful, while betting as a bluff risks losing only one bet when unsuccessful. When taken together, however, these two plays are simply revealing too much information about your hand; and against an observant opponent, you soon wouldn't be able to make either of them with success.[33]

You cannot therefore expect to be successful in a poker game against good, experienced opponents by making only "range of the moment" decisions for when to bluff, to value bet, to slowplay, and so on.[34] Instead, you must come into the game with an intelligently pre-prepared strategy for exactly how you will play each of your hands in each distinct situation, so that you can coordinate your plays for all of the hands you can—and in the long run *will*—have in a certain situation with one another, thereby making sure that you aren't giving away easy reads and profitable opportunities to your opponents.

In addition, you have to pay attention not only to *which* plays you are going make in a certain situation, but also with what frequency you are going to make them. That is, even if you bluff and bet for value in the same manner, you can still betray a valuable read to your opponents if you are bluffing in a certain spot too often or not often enough. Sklansky illustrates this concept well in *The Theory of Poker*:

> Imagine that you are up against an opponent who on the last round bets $20 into a $100 pot. You are getting 6-to-1 from the pot if you call. However, you know you can only win, as is often

---

[33] Against an oblivious opponent, however, you can make both of these plays with impunity and maximize your expectation in each case, with him being none the wiser.

[34] To "slowplay" means: To play a strong hand weakly (and thus disguise the strength of your hand).

the case, if your opponent is bluffing. Let's say you know three opponents well. The first never bluffs in this spot, so your response to that player's bet is easy: You fold with full knowledge that you have not cost yourself any money. The second opponent frequently bluffs. Once again your response is easy: You call, knowing you are going to win that last bet so often that calling must result in a long-run profit. The third player is the problem. He bets in such a way that the odds are about 6-to-1 against his bluffing. . . .

Now you have a tough decision. You must choose between two equally upsetting alternatives. . . . If you fold, you know there's a chance your opponent stole the pot from you; but if you call, you know that six times out of seven you are simply donating your money to your opponent. Thus, a person who bluffs with approximately the right frequency . . . is a much better poker player and will win much more money in the long run than a person who virtually never bluffs or a person who bluffs too much.

This consequently requires that you know with what frequencies you will have *your* various hands in each distinct situation, so that you can then mix your bluffs in with your value bets, and your slowplays in with your straightforward checks/calls, in the exact proportions that will make you the most money in the long run. And there is in fact an optimal proportion, dictated by *game theory*, with which to combine these plays. Sklansky explains this concept well in relation to bluffing:

Mathematically, optimal bluffing strategy is to bluff in such a way that the chances against your bluffing are identical to the pot odds your opponent is getting. Thus, if, as in the example just given, an opponent is getting 6-to-1 from the pot, the chances against your bluffing should be 6-to-1. Then that opponent would break even on the last bet by calling every time and also by folding every time. If he called, he would lose $20 six times and win $120 once; if he folded, he would win nothing and lose nothing. Regardless of what your opponent does, you average winning an extra $100 every seven hands.

So, if you know that in a certain situation you will have a strong hand—with which you will value bet—60% of the time, you should ideally also bluff in that spot with the weakest 10% of your hands (if your opponent is getting 6-to-1 odds to call) as a way of maximizing your expectation (against a good opponent) through the use of deception.[35]

What all this means is that you essentially have to *read your own hand*—the same way your observant opponents will—and in each distinct situation determine what hands you can have, with what frequency you will have them, and what plays you will make with them, in order to construct a strategy that will employ the perfect amount of deception, and thereby be the most profitable against your good, technically sound opponents.

WHERE SKLANSKY'S INSTRUCTION BREAKS DOWN

It was here that my exclusively categorical approach to hand reading broke down altogether. It was impossible, using this method, to determine the precise frequencies with which I would hold my various types of hands in various situations. Exactly like reading an opponent's hand, and for the same reasons, it only allowed me to guess at these frequencies by way of vague, imprecise estimates from experience. It *did* work fairly well for reading an opponent's hand, when using deception wasn't required; and it could work equally well for employing deception, when reading the opponent's hand wasn't required. But in situations that required *both*, those that necessitated making a two-sided evaluation of the hands my opponents could hold and their probabilities, and the hands I could have and their

---

[35] Sklansky explained this concept of the optimal bluffing frequency very well in his section on game theory (page 179) in *The Theory of Poker*, which was perhaps the most valuable part of the book—at least for me when I first read it.

probabilities, as well as then weighing and balancing these against one another, the imprecise estimates I could make through categorical hand reading proved totally inadequate.

The result was that even though I perfectly *understood* the mathematical concepts behind deception, expectation, hand reading, and so forth, I was nevertheless left to construct the overall strategies by which I played poker (what I then referred to as my "game") not from my own personal calculations of the optimal strategy for each particular scenario, but from the strict categorical rules that I obtained from various poker books and authors. And this, really, is a good summation of the effect David Sklansky's books had on me. They certainly gave me a better understanding of the game and taught me the fundamental mathematical principles behind every poker decision. But because of the two inescapable problems that came with categorical hand reading—the first being that I was unable to adequately determine the probability that my opponent would have a certain hand in a certain situation, and the second being that I couldn't even adequately determine the probability that *I* would have a certain hand in a certain situation—my actual decision making at the poker table was still largely dictated by the same kind of strict categorical rules as when I had little to no understanding of the game at all. After all, knowing the math to apply in a situation does little good when you cannot properly determine the numbers you need to make the requisite calculations.

There was, however, one major area of the game in which Sklansky's books and the mathematical concepts I learned from them *did* have a profound effect on my decision making, and drastically improved my results. These were the situations in which hand reading—either of my own hand, my opponents' hands, or both—was largely unnecessary or inconsequential. For instance, in hands where I had the nuts,[36] or close to it, or a draw to the same, I could calculate my chances of winning without even considering my opponents' hands, since my

---

[36] The current best hand possible, given the cards on the board.

cards beat (or would beat) practically all of their possible holdings. Similarly, in hands where the pot was already very large in proportion to future bets, in hands with four or more players in the pot, and in hands against bad and inexperienced opponents, the need to employ deception generally went out the window, and therefore absolved me from having to read my own hands.

In many such situations, I really could calculate the expectation for each of my available plays, and *dynamically* decide on the best course of action without reference to any poker books. In these hands, math could be said to dictate the correct play much more than judgment. And I was fully capable of performing all the mathematical calculations in any hand, as long as I didn't have to make a profusion of crude probability estimates from experience.

As for Sklansky's part, he very lucidly and comprehensibly explained all such situations in which math primarily dictated the correct play. Here, for example, is how he describes a purely mathematical situation in his extraordinarily insightful book, *Small Stakes Hold'em: Winning Big with Expert Play*:

> **You are on the button with A♥8♥. The player under the gun [first to act] raises, and four people cold-call. You call. Both blinds also call (16 small bets [in the pot]). The flop is T♥9♥2♠, giving you the nut [best possible] flush draw. The small blind bets, the big blind calls, and the preflop raiser raises. Two more players call, and the other two fold (24 small bets [in the pot]). What should you do?**

> **Answer:** Reraise. You have a big draw to the nuts [the best hand possible]. By the river, you will make the nut flush 35 percent of the time, and you will sometimes win by just spiking an ace. With five remaining opponents, you will win far more often than seventeen percent of the time, so you have a huge pot equity edge. Reraise for value.

For hands in which *judgment* primarily determined the correct play, however, Sklansky took a more authoritative approach. Here's an example from the same book, where he so eloquently described a collection of primarily mathematical situations, of a hand in which *judgment* mainly dictates the correct play:

> You have J♥5♦ in the big blind. Two players limp, the small blind calls, and you check (4 small bets). The flop is J♣8♣3♥, giving you top pair. The small blind checks, and you bet. The first limper folds, but the second raises. The small blind folds, and you call (4 big bets). The turn is the 9♠. You check, and your opponent bets. What should you do?
>
> **Answer:** Fold. You bet the flop because there was a strong chance that you had the best hand. While you did not have a strong kicker, any top pair will often be the best hand in a four-way, unraised pot. When raised, you cannot like your hand much anymore. It is likely that you are behind to a jack with a stronger kicker. Even if you are ahead, your opponent probably has a decent draw (e.g., a flush draw, perhaps also with an overcard to your jacks). So you will rarely outdraw your opponent if behind but he will outdraw you relatively often if you are ahead.
>
> You might fold immediately to a flop raise, but there are a few reasons to call.... No matter what [however], you should give up on the turn when you do not improve, and your opponent bets. *Calling down with probable second-best hands in small pots is not profitable.*

Notice that the main reason Sklansky gives for folding top pair in this situation is that there's too great a chance the opponent has an even better top pair (with a higher kicker). If the opponent does have that hand, you'll only have about a 6.5% chance of winning (by catching one of the three remaining fives) by the river. On the other hand, if the opponent has a flush draw with an overcard, as Sklansky says is the most likely other alternative, you'll have about a 74% chance of still having the strongest hand at the end. Since you're effectively getting 3-to-1 odds in this situation (you have to call two big bets on the turn and the river to win what will be six big bets in total), in order for folding to be correct here, the opponent must have a jack with a higher kicker (or an even better hand) in this spot more than 73% of the time.[37]

Sklansky's hand reading here argues that this indeed is the case. Since you bet in this spot against three opponents (each of whom could have picked up a playable hand), your bet is very unlikely to win the pot immediately, and is therefore probably not a bluff. Thus, your bet here announces you have a pretty strong hand. And since the opponent sees this and still raises you, his raise indicates an even stronger hand, probably top pair or a flush draw.

But can't the opponent do this with a weaker hand like middle pair, bottom pair, or even ace-high? Well, sure he can. But the core principle here is that even if he does, and causes you to fold your top pair in this spot as a result, you — or one of the other players — will pick up an *even stronger* hand with which to call or reraise him in the same spot often enough to make raising with those hands unprofitable for him in the long run. Thus, because the only hands the opponent could profitably raise with here are strong draws or hands top pair or better (and presumably he will have those hands more than 73% of the time and draws less than 27% of the time), folding your top pair here is the correct play.

---

[37] Your chance of catching a five on the last card is 3/46 (the three remaining fives out of 46 unknown cards), or about 6.5%. And your opponent's chance of catching a flush or a pair higher than jacks on the last card is 12/46 (the nine remaining clubs, plus the three high cards that will give him a higher pair, out of the 46 unknown cards in the deck), or about 24%. For your expectation here to be negative, then, with your 3-to-1 odds, your overall probability of winning has to be less than 25% — for which you must have your 6.5% chance of winning at least 73% of the time, and your 76% chance of winning at most 27% of the time: (6.5% * 73%) + (76% * 27%) = 25%.

Well, this is certainly sound hand reading. But do notice that every assumption about probability here is a pure rationalization, tailored to support the initial assumption that folding in this spot really *is* the correct play. The fact is that with just this kind of categorical hand reading (as we will soon see), there's absolutely no way to determine what the probability that the opponent actually has any of these hands is.

And yet, I accepted the play in this example—and many others like it—as undoubtedly *correct*. I made them into categorical rules that I would then follow, with confidence, when a similar situation came up in my own play—all the while rationalizing to myself that the math *must be there*, even though I had no way to verify it.

Meanwhile, Sklansky's books (as well as those by other authors) were chock full of these kinds of examples. And for all situations where I found my own judgment and experience insufficient, I hungrily turned to these books for a similar practice hand, to find what the "correct" play in that spot really was, and to then turn it into a categorical rule to abide by in the future. In these situations, I was essentially deferring my judgment to that of the poker authors, who I considered to possess the wealth of experience that I lacked—and to therefore know for certain what hands a typical opponent will have, and with what frequency, in situations where I simply did not.

THE JUDGMENT-MATH DICHOTOMY

There therefore emerged, at this point in my poker development, a peculiar kind of dichotomy in my game. In situations where *math* primarily dictated the correct strategy and little to no judgment was required, I no longer needed to play by a strict set of categorical rules I extracted from poker books. In these situations, I was now fully able to make my decision independently: by dynamically calculating the expectation of each available play myself, and simply choosing the one with the highest expectation. In situations where selecting the correct play was ultimately a matter of judgment, however, I still often made my decisions categorically, by following a strict set of categorical rules that I collected from various poker books, which provided me with a default correct play for each specific type of situation.

I should note, however, that as I played more and more poker and increasingly gained more first-hand experience with it, my judgment and hand reading really did improve. But this improvement had a starkly different effect on the two dichotomized parts of my game.

In the part of the game where I *could* dynamically calculate the correct play in a hand, my play became even *more* dynamic. My increased experience allowed me to make better and more accurate estimates while reading hands, and I became able to calculate the correct play independently in an increasing number of situations. In the small and medium stakes Limit Hold'em games I primarily played in, such situations came up about 50% of the time, and I truly became able, in Sklansky's words, to "squeeze every last penny of value" out of them.

However, in the areas of the game where I *couldn't* dynamically calculate the correct play in a hand, my play became even *more* categorical. As Sklansky put it, "in hold'em, an almost infinite number of unique situations and possibilities can occur," and the more I played, the more I encountered these *unique* situations, for which the categorical rules I had already acquired couldn't tell me the correct play. Some of these situations fell into two (or more) categories at once, each indicating a different play. And others couldn't be placed in a category at all.

When I encountered these situations, I hungrily leafed through my poker books for a similar practice hand, to find out what the "correct" play in that spot really was, and then made it into a categorical rule to abide by in the future. As a result, the categories I played by continuously grew both in their number and specificity, so that by the end of two years, I had well over two hundred different categories to orchestrate my gameplay. All of these were, of course, situated within a comprehensive general strategy that at least attempted to mix deception and straightforward play in optimal proportions, and that truly *did* make me a highly dangerous player to be up against.

THE LAB

In addition to simply spending a greater amount of time at the poker table, I also gained experience and worked on refining my game (the entire categorical system by which I played poker) in private, in what I jokingly called "the lab." The lab consisted of me dealing out nine hands (the number of players at a full poker table) in front of me on my desk or bed, and seeing how the deal unfolded when I played each hand the way I would've if I didn't know what any of the other hands were. This was something I learned from my father, who was also an avid poker player. And it was of tremendous help in allowing me to see all my categorical rules in action, from both sides of the hand. I could then refine my game by picking out the rules that led me to a good decision most of the time, and throw out the ones that did not. I would often joke to my friends (who all thought this was quite amusing) that the lab gave me nine times as much experience as playing in a real game, since in each round I played all of the nine hands myself. (It was at least partially true.)

ON THE VERGE

And so, for about two years after I read my first poker book, I devoted myself entirely to the game. I would spend nearly all my free time, five or six hours each day, playing poker online or in school, laying out cards in the lab, watching the multimillion-dollar poker tournaments on television, and reading every poker book I could get my hands on. The result was that, after those two years, I became quite a savvy and experienced poker player. And I constantly worked at perfecting, separately, the two dichotomized parts of my game.

Despite the substantial improvements in my "game" and poker earnings, however, I remained acutely aware of the unsettling incongruity between the mathematical aspect of poker and its judgment aspect. Although my ability to read hands improved steadily with experience, it still bothered me greatly that this half of the game lacked that same crisp mathematical certainty and unassailable logic that ruled its other half. This discontent was further exacerbated when I also began playing No Limit Hold'em, where judgment plays a much greater role (since the pots can never really be large in comparison with the bets, and most hands are contested between just two players).

As an extension of this, I felt uneasy with the part of my game in which categories orchestrated my decision making, since I could not be entirely sure that the math behind many of these categories was correct. This was as opposed to the part of the game in which I *could* personally make all of the necessary calculations, and therefore knew the exact mathematical reasons for every play that I made. Nevertheless, I mostly resigned myself to the idea that this was simply an unavoidable part of poker; and that the only way I would eventually overcome this deficiency was by "refining my game" (that is, making the categorical rules I played by more numerous and specific), as well as acquiring several additional years of experience.

And then, I read Harrington on Hold'em.

Part Two: A New Method of Thinking

The *Harrington on Hold'em* series dealt exclusively with No Limit Hold'em—a version of the game that has a different set of betting rules, and is therefore an altogether different kind of poker from the Limit Hold'em I was primarily versed in. For those first two years, perhaps 90% of all the games I played in were Limit Hold'em. And as I was now learning to play No Limit, which was essentially a new game that I had very little experience with, I hungered for a new set of categorical rules (like I had for Limit Hold'em) to direct my play and replace the helplessness I often experienced when I encountered a hand I had simply no answer for. I hoped *Harrington on Hold'em* would provide this.

Now the first two volumes in the series certainly *did* serve as a fertile source for the categorical rules I desired. In fact, they became the main staple of my No Limit Hold'em game (in the infrequent occasions I ventured to play it). And this *did* yield generally positive results. Nevertheless, I was still a relative novice at the game and knew that I had a lot more work to do before I could play it at an expert level. So, when the third volume of *Harrington on Hold'em* came out in the summer of 2006, I eagerly ordered a copy in hopes of improving my game.

At first, I noticed nothing extraordinary about the book. Like most other poker books, it employed the familiar medium of practice hands. In fact, it consisted entirely of practice hands, fifty of them in total, spanning the just over three-hundred-page length of the book. "This book is laid out as a big quiz," Harrington wrote in its introduction. The reader was invited to answer its practice hands on his own, then to compare his answers to Harrington's *correct* ones, and to finally tally up his total score based on the number of questions he got right.

Having already read Harrington's first two volumes, and figuring this one to be mostly a test of the things I had learned there, I was highly confident that I would receive a near perfect score. To my surprise, however, many of the plays Harrington proclaimed correct in this volume differed considerably from those he endorsed in the first two. And many of the explanations he gave for these *new* plays, seemed to entirely contradict what he wrote in those previous volumes. Needless to say, I wound up with an abysmally low score.

HARRINGTON'S HURDLES

Thus, Harrington's third book puzzled and frustrated me. In the first place, it seemed to contain a wealth of new, useful knowledge. The plays Harrington was advocating here, I thought, really were the correct ones. And in order to improve my No-Limit Hold'em game, I needed to assimilate them into my own play. Simultaneously, however, I was utterly unable to understand Harrington's reasoning behind these new strategies. And this left me in the same basic position of accepting an author's *conclusions* as correct, not understanding why they were correct, and being nevertheless compelled to categorize them into a strict set of rules to play by in the future.

In trying to do so, however, I soon found that the practice hands in Harrington's book were simply too few (just fifty in total) and too different from one another to form any broad categorical rules out of—I could not determine how broadly such a rule was to be applied or where to draw its limits. I would lay out hands in the lab to test the plays the book advocated, and I would continually discover that it offered no definitive answer for how to play in the vast majority of situations. I created some tentative categories and rules from the practice hands in the book, but when I then implemented them at an actual poker table, I would very frequently wind up in ambiguous situations in which I simply didn't know what play to make. As a result, I often ended up making the wrong plays, and my No-Limit Hold'em game began hemorrhaging money.

Perhaps I was missing some crucial idea in this book, I thought. Having allowed enough time to pass that I didn't simply remember the answer to each problem, I reread the book from cover to cover, and was again surprised that I still got most of its questions wrong.

Clearly, I *was* missing something, but I couldn't tell what. I reread the first two volumes in the series hoping to gain some perspective, but this only made the contradictions between them and this third book stand out in even sharper contrast. What I didn't realize at the time was that this third volume was fundamentally different from any of the other poker books I read. And the practice hands in it were different as well.

Every other poker author I read (including Harrington in his first two books) employed practice hands primarily as a way to "teach by example." It was a way to instruct the reader what the "correct" plays were in various situations by illustrating those plays using hypothetical scenarios. The reasons they gave to support those plays were therefore of secondary importance, short, and often *ad hoc*. "Working through these [practice] hands will develop your ability to determine the correct play at the table," said one of Sklansky's books, "You will encounter situations similar to those in our quizzes, recall our analysis, and identify the correct play." In this third book, however, Harrington used his practice hands not as a way of teaching the reader how to *play* in various specific situations, but as a way of teaching him how to *think* during the decision-making process in general. It was for this reason that the third book contained only fifty practice hands, while others easily fit hundreds. Harrington devoted six pages on average, and for many hands twice that, to an in-depth analysis of each individual practice hand, and the decision-making process behind it. (This was as opposed to the at most two or three pages, and usually only half or a third of a page, that the other books devoted to their primarily illustrative practice hands.)

What was essentially happening, although I didn't realize it at the time, was that the categorical method of learning, thinking, and making decisions with which I approached life in general and poker in particular rendered me completely incapable of assimilating the information in Harrington's third book. It was, after all, expounding an entirely different method of thinking from my categorical one. Oblivious to this fact, however, I only redoubled my efforts to categorize the book's practice hands. I thought that if I just put in the additional effort and read into the book more diligently, I would somehow be able to fit everything in Harrington's three volumes together and ultimately end up with a sound, comprehensive system of play.

And so, I read the book for a third time.

GLIMMER

The white sky glared outside my sixth-floor bedroom window, around one in the afternoon, on a cloudy weekend in November 2006. (It may have been my Thanksgiving week off from school.) I lay on my bed, propped up on my elbows, my neck crooked over the final pages of the third volume of *Harrington on Hold'em*. I flipped its last leaf from right to left and closed the book shut. I pushed it away.

Thrice now I had read this book, and again I had gotten a large batch of the answers to its practice hands incorrect. It now seemed to me that I was no closer to understanding the things Harrington was trying to convey in it than I was upon the first reading. It just made no sense to me. Harrington's first two books were perfectly reasonable, and I absorbed their contents with ease. Why, then, could I not tally the things he wrote in this third book, which also seemed reasonable, with those other two? I was again left with a feeling of general uncertainty, along with a distinct tinge of frustration at the contradictions I seemed to be encountering on its pages. Nevertheless, I set to trying to work it out.

I sat up from my bed and reached over to a table for a deck of red-shelled cards. I shuffled them a few times and began dealing out hands on the bed. I was entering "the lab" for yet another attempt at consolidating Harrington's teachings into a coherent system of categorical rules.

I let each "lab" deal play out the way it would at an actual poker table; that is, if I sat in every seat and played every hand without seeing the others. While doing so, I tried to match the random situations that came up and in which I was uncertain about the correct play with a similar practice hand from Harrington's book, in order to see how each hand would play out if I followed his advice. Again, I butted up against the same problem I had earlier. Few hands matched up precisely to the examples in the book, and there remained a large aspect of ambiguity as to which play, according to the book, was the correct one in the majority of situations. I went through ten or twenty deals in this way, my frustration at the inadequacy of Harrington's book steadily growing. And then, I dealt the following hand:

In one of the middle positions I ended up with A-A, in the small blind I held 6-6. Preflop I raised to 3 times the big blind with the aces and called that raise with the sixes, as is the standard play with both of those hands. In all of the other positions the hands were too weak to play, and I folded them. The flop was Q-6-2, with no flush draws available. The course of action to take with the sixes was obvious. Since they now made a set (three of a kind), a virtually unbeatable hand on this flop, the goal was to get as much money into the pot as possible—which in No Limit Hold'em is always as much money as you have in front of you. The difficulty was with the aces. These were also an extremely strong hand on this flop, but not an unbeatable one. And in this case, of course, they were *already* beaten.

The dilemma was: Is there, if this were a real situation, any way for me to figure out that the opponent had my aces beat and fold them without losing all my money? This wasn't a problem that existed in Limit Hold'em. There the most I could lose with aces was several bets; and there are a variety of hands, many of them losing to aces, that the opponent could make those bets with. In No Limit, however, all the chips I have in front of me are at risk. And there is always the question of whether the opponent would move all his chips into the pot in this situation with any hand that *didn't* have the aces beat. It was essentially a problem of hand reading.

This dilemma is a common one in No Limit Hold'em: where a player with a great hand that is not the nuts butts up against an opponent who holds the actual nuts, and is forced to make a decision for his entire stack. Some very good players in these situations are frequently able to deduce that their opponents are holding the pure nuts and fold their strong but second-best hands. This was, of course, a skill I was aspiring to. And Harrington's third book contained several examples of precisely this kind of decision. In this situation with the aces against sixes, however, neither the book nor my hand reading experience could offer an answer.

I looked through Harrington's book for a corresponding example to this situation, but once again I failed to find any. I would have loved to find among Harrington's practice hands a ready-made judgment, as was often provided in Sklansky's and other poker books, for precisely this kind of scenario—where Harrington would say something like: 'You are clearly beat here: Fold,' or 'You cannot get away from this hand, if your opponent is fortunate enough to have you beat, you're just going to have to lose all your money'—but of course there was none. Nonetheless, I kept leafing through Harrington's third book for at least some clue for how to play the aces in this spot. I stopped on one practice hand in which the only similarity to my current problem was that one player raised around the same amount in early position and another called that raise in the small blind.

I read through that hand again, but felt like I was grasping at straws, futilely searching for a solution that simply wasn't there. Not only did this hand offer no answer to my current predicament, even in its own context the things Harrington wrote about it seemed to me odd and beside the point. In what I can best describe as a kind of angry desperation, and in part as a way of mocking Harrington's book, I made a deliberate attempt to follow his instructions in that hand word-for-word, as if to prove to myself that there was simply no sense to be made of it.

"Your first job," Harrington wrote, "is to start thinking about the hands he might have used to call. Top players try to be very specific at this stage. You don't want to fall into the habit of thinking 'He called, so maybe he has something.' Instead, you want to narrow his range down to some reasonable group of hands."

"Okay," I thought sarcastically; "but how do I tell what hands he could have!? All he did was call a small raise preflop: *He could have anything!*" My frustration with Harrington's book was really reaching a boiling point. And then, a new idea suddenly dawned on me: With what hands would *I* have made that play in my opponent's position?

My anger instantly melted away and was replaced by a kind of eager excitement. After all, I knew *exactly* how to play preflop with every single hand, from every single position, in response to every possible action my opponents could take—Harrington's books (as well as every other instructional poker book) provided this directly.[38] And I had long since absorbed and assimilated that information into my own game. When I tried to read my opponents' hands, however, I didn't think so specifically in terms of which individual hands would be profitable for them in that situation. I simply thought, as Harrington so aptly warned against: 'He probably has a pretty strong hand,' or 'he most likely has a couple high cards,' and so forth. That is a clear hallmark of categorical thinking.

Now I discovered that I could resolve this incongruity between the way I played my own hands and the way I read my opponents' by essentially putting myself in their shoes. "If you had one of those hands [in your opponent's position], would *you* call a bet?" Harrington had written elsewhere in the volume. And indeed, by imagining myself in my opponent's position (which wasn't hard to do, especially since in the lab I physically *was* my opponent) I could arrive at a well-defined list of specific, *individual* hands that a player making that call in that situation could actually have. What this effectively accomplished was reducing the hand categories I formerly thought in—i.e. *a strong hand, a mediocre hand, a weak hand*; or alternately *high cards, a small pocket pair, suited connectors,* and so forth—into the individual items, the hands, that comprised them. And once I did that, the issue of the *frequencies* with which the opponent could have each of those hands was also resolved. Harrington was very explicit about this:

"We know there are 1,326 possible poker hands (52 times 51 divided by 2)," Harrington had already written in his second volume, "Once two cards are removed [the two in your hand] the remaining fifty cards form only 1,225 hands. For every pair, there are six possible ways of dealing the pair. For every non-pair, there are 16 possible

---

[38] Recall the *"Starting Requirements"* chart on page 18.

ways of dealing the hand, 12 unsuited and four suited." Thus, once you read your opponents' hands in terms of *individual hands* rather than *hand categories*, all the uncertainty about the frequencies of those hands is eliminated. Each individual hand has a precise probability of being dealt.

Before your opponent takes any action at all, he can be holding any one of 1,225 unique two-card combinations. The chance he has specifically A-K offsuit (or any other offsuit, non-pair hand) then is 12/1,225 or 0.98%. The chance he has A-K suited (or any other suited hand) is 4/1,225. The chance he has A-A (or any other pair) is 6/1,225. You can be even more precise about these probabilities by accounting for the cards you know your opponent cannot hold—this includes the cards in your hand, the cards that are dealt on the board, and any cards the dealer or another player inadvertently flips over, letting you know that your present opponent could not have possibly been dealt them. Thus, if you have an ace in your hand preflop, the chance your opponent could be dealt A-K (suited or unsuited) is 12/1,225 instead of 16, because there are now only 12 possible combinations of three aces and four kings as opposed to 16. And the chance that he is dealt A-A is now 3/1,225, since there remain only three combinations of A-A that can be made from the three remaining aces. Of course if you had two aces in your hand, the chance your opponent now has A-K (or any other A-x hand) is 6/1,225. And the chance he has specifically A-A (the two remaining aces) is only 1/1,225.

From that starting point, I could proceed with my hand reading as I normally did, narrowing down the range of hands my opponent could hold based on his actions. Only now, instead of thinking exclusively in terms of the *categories* of hands he could have, I could break those categories down into their individual hand constituents. So, if the board is something like A-T-8 and I want to know what the chance is that my opponent has top pair, I could clarify that question into: "What is the probability he has exactly A-K, A-Q, A-J, A-9, A-7, A-6, A-5, A-4, A-3, or A-2?" To then determine which of those individual hands he could actually have, I would put myself in his shoes and ask: "If I were in that player's position, which of these hands would I have made all the same plays with?" Because I knew *from experience* that the plays my opponent made would have been profitable, for example, with A-K, A-Q, A-J, and A-9, but not with A-7 or lower; I could conclude that, if he is a competent player, he can only have top pair with those four highest Ace-x hands, but not with the lowest six—a total of 48 possible combinations.[39] Of course, if he is an incompetent player, he certainly could be holding A-7 or lower in that spot: But once again, the core principle here is that *if* he did have those hands, he would have been playing them unprofitably, which would be more to his detriment in the long run than whatever he'd gain from the error caused in my calculations as a result.[40]

BREAKTHROUGH

It took me no more than a few minutes to realize all this. In that unexpected moment of insight, I suddenly understood everything Harrington had written in his third book. It all rushed through my mind and came together into a clear, comprehensive *method*. All of my uncertainties about hand reading and about poker in general seemed to me instantly resolved by this new approach.

I had the distinct feeling of having stumbled onto something huge, something terribly important; as if I had just discovered the key to all the poker problems I had been struggling with for the past two years. A great sense of excitement was rising inside me. My mind and even my vision felt sharper, my thoughts much more clear, much more distinct. I looked down at the cards still lying on my bed. A queen, a six, and a two were lying face up, staring back at me. Two hands—the aces and the sixes—were lying face down on either side of them.

With still a measure of caution—I was not yet entirely sure it would work—I now applied my newly discovered method to the current problem.

---

[39] There are 12 possible ways to make each of those four hands, since one of the aces in the deck is already on the board.
[40] This is simply an extension of game theory.

In middle position the aces (let's call this *Player* 1) raised to three-times the big blind. In the small blind the sixes (let's call this *Player* 2) called that raise. Everyone else folded. The flop came Q-6-2, all different suits. I now asked myself: What are all the hands I could have called that 3x raise with in *Player 2's* position? Answer:

- Any pocket pair.
- Any suited connector from 8-7 to K-Q.
- Any A-x suited, from A-K to A-2.
- A-K offsuit, A-Q offsuit, A-J offsuit, K-Q offsuit, K-J suited, K-T suited, and Q-T suited.

Now, with the flop coming Q-6-2, *Player* 2 absolutely must check his set of sixes. That is because this kind of flop—with no draws and only one high card—will in the long run miss most two-card hands. If checked to, *Player* 1 will therefore bet no matter what he has (poker players call this a "continuation bet") in hopes of winning the pot right there; which is of course perfect for *Player* 2, who now wants his opponent to commit as much money as possible to the pot. This is the standard play of "checking to the preflop raiser."

So *Player* 2 checks, and *Player* 1 bets half the pot—a standard size for a continuation bet in No Limit Hold'em. With everything going according to plan, *Player* 2 now has to raise with his trip-sixes and try to get all of *Player 1's* money into the pot. In all lab hands, I was assuming each player started with 100 times the big blind in his stack. My main question here was: If *Player* 2 simply pushed all-in at this point, would I in *Player 1's* position ever be able to fold my A-A? I continued my analysis:

Again, the next step was dividing *Player 2's* possible hands into categories. Here I only needed two categories: (1) Hands that beat me, and (2) Hands that lost to me. The only hands that beat A-A at this point were two-pairs (with Q-6, Q-2, and 6-2) and three of a kind (with Q-Q, 6-6, and 2-2). All other hands lost to me, consisting of (1) Pocket pairs that missed the flop, (2) Non-pair hands that made one pair on the flop, and (3) Non-pair hands that didn't make a pair on the flop. To determine the probability of each of these categories, then, I needed to reduce them to their individual hands, count the number of their combinations, and estimate how likely I would have been to call the preflop raise with each of them:

- Two pair (Q-6, Q-2, and 6-2)—I wouldn't be caught dead playing any of those hands preflop against a raise. Total: *0 combinations.*

- Trips (Q-Q, 6-6, and 2-2)—I would usually reraise with QQ in this position, but *sometimes* I could call to "vary my play." In a similar situation Harrington recommended: "With Queens . . . reraise 70% [of the time] and call 30%." So I might just call with the Queens in this position one third of the time: *3 combinations * 33% = 1 combination.* With the sixes I would certainly make that call preflop: *3 combinations.* And although I would usually just fold the twos, I might mix in a call perhaps one third of the time to vary my play: *1 combination.* Total: *5 combinations.*

- Pocket pairs that missed the flop—With pocket nines, eights, sevens and fives I would call preflop almost 100% of the time: *24 combinations.* With Jacks and Tens I would call perhaps 25% of the time and reraise 75%: *3 combinations.* With Aces and Kings I would call perhaps 15% of the time and reraise 85%: *1 combination.* (Remember, there is only one remaining combination of aces.) With threes and fours I would fold perhaps 66% of the time and call 33% of the time: *4 combinations.* Total: *32 combinations.*

- Non-pair hands that missed the flop—With A-K I would call perhaps 25% of the time and reraise 75%: *2 combinations.* (Remember I am performing this analysis from *Player 1's* perspective and know that two of the aces are unavailable.) I would nearly always make the call with A-J: *8 combinations.* Same goes for A-T suited, K-J suited, and K-T suited: *10 combinations.* Same for every suited connector J-T to 8-7: *16 combinations.* And also for A-3 to A-5 suited: *6 combinations.* And I would call perhaps 50% of the time and fold the other 50% with A-7 suited to A-9 suited: *3 combinations.* Total: *45 combinations.*

- Non-pair hands that made one pair on the flop—With A-Q, I
  would call virtually every time: *6 combinations*. Same for K-Q: *12
  combinations*. I would also call with Q-J suited and Q-T suited: *6
  combinations*. The same goes for A-2 suited: *2 combinations*. And I
  would call maybe 50% of the time with A-6 suited: *1 combination*.
  Total: *27 combinations*.

Thus, before *Player 2* check-raised all-in, he could have about 109 possible combinations—5 of which beat me and 104 of which lose to me. The next thing I want to know is: Which of these hands could he have made the all-in check-raise with? Putting myself in his shoes no longer helps here, because I would *never* make that play with any kind of hand. To go all-in here, *Player 2* would have to push in his remaining 97 times the big blind to win a pot that currently has only 10.5 times the big blind in it.[41] Such a gross overbet is of course a completely novice move—one that a good player would almost never make. So if *Player 2* goes all-in here, from *Player 1's* perspective, he looks to have made a very odd play no matter what he's holding.

Still, there are some reasons for a person to make this bet. He could of course have a monster hand—I would say either trips, A-Q, or K-K in this situation—and hope the opponent calls him to take his entire stack. This is the most likely scenario. The second most likely scenario is that he is simply bluffing. The all-in here provides a terrible win-to-lose ratio for a bluff, which has to make the opponent fold more than 90% of the time to make a profit, but a novice might make this type of move out of desperation. The most unlikely scenario is that he has a mediocre hand like a top pair or middle pair, which would make the all-in here an absolutely terrible move, since it will only be called if that hand is beat. Still, *Player 2* might make this play if he is a complete maniac.

To be extremely cautious here, we can estimate that *Player 2* will make this play 100% of the time with three of a kind, *5 combinations;*

---

[41] Player 1's 3x preflop raise, Player 2's call of that raise, the folded big blind, and Player 1's 3.5 BB continuation bet.

50% of the time with K-K, *0.5 combinations*; and 25% of the time with A-Q, *2 combinations*. So, if he is making a value bet here, there is a 5-to-2 ratio he is beating me. Of his remaining 102 combinations, he will have a pair with 57 of them, and absolutely nothing with 45 of them. What then is the chance that he will make the all-in move here with any of these hands? Harrington offered an easy solution to this in his first volume:

> **Harrington's Law of Bluffing:** The probability that your opponent is bluffing when he shoves a big bet into the pot is always at least 10 percent. At least 10 percent! It may be higher, but it won't be lower. Why not? Because people bluff. They know they're supposed to bluff, they like the thrill of pulling off an outrageous bluff, so sometimes they do bluff. You've seen it happen all the time on television, and it will happen in your hands too.

That makes it absolutely clear! If the opponent bluffs just 10% of the time with his remaining 102 hands, that is an average of 10.2 combinations, which alone outnumbers the hands that beat me here by more than double. Even if I assumed that this opponent would *never* bluff here with a pair (an unreasonable assumption), and only do so with the 45 combinations with which he has absolutely nothing, this *still* yields a whopping 4.5 combinations. In the worst-case scenario, then, there is a 6.5-to-5 chance that I have the opponent beat.

If I do have him beat, my A-A has about a 90% chance on average of remaining best by the river. If has me beat with a set, my A-A has about a 10% chance to win by catching a third ace by the river. Thus, I will win 90% of the time against the 6.5 combinations I am beating (5.85 combinations) and 10% of the time against the 5 combinations I am losing to (0.5 combinations), for a total average of 6.35 wins out of 11.5 trials—or just over a 55% chance of winning the pot. Since the pot is offering 107.5-to-93.5 odds, which means that I only need a 46.5% chance of winning to break even, this turns out to be an easy call!

In conclusion, by calculating the frequencies of each individual hand in this manner, it becomes absolutely clear that the probability of the opponent hitting a set here is just so miniscule that it is correct to call his all-in on the sole likelihood that he might be bluffing. And this is something that would be completely unrecognizable through categorical hand reading alone.[42]

Harrington also understood that this approach was different from the categorical hand reading described by Sklansky. And so, he called this method not merely *hand reading*, but *"Structured Hand Analysis,"* or alternately, *Range of Hand Analysis*. "If this seems like an intimidating amount of work to do for a single hand," Harrington warned of this method, "don't be discouraged. It is a fair amount of work, but it gets much easier with a little practice." "And if you ever wondered just what good players are thinking when they pause for a long time," he continued, "well, they're thinking pretty much like this."

REDUCING CATEGORIES TO REALITY, FIRSTHAND EXPERIENCE, AND THE COMPREHENSIVE METHOD

Having completed this analysis, I shuffled all the cards back into the deck and put it off to the side. I felt completely in awe before what I had just discovered. From the murk and uncertainty I was experiencing only moments earlier, I had just reached a perfectly clear and unambiguous solution to what had seemed to me a completely intractable problem. The two key features of this new approach, which are so important that I must restate them here, were:

1) Reducing *hand categories* to individual hands.
2) Deciding how an opponent would play those hands based on the way *I* would play them in his position.

The difference between thinking in individual hands instead of hand categories struck me like the difference between day and night. This

---

[42] Those familiar with statistics will also recognize this as a direct application of *Bayes Theorem*.

wasn't merely a matter of thinking more specifically as opposed to more generally, but of thinking on the level of *reality* as opposed to the level of *empty abstractions*.

It was always implicitly obvious to me that a category of hand such as *top pair* stood for, and was a summary of, all the individual hands with which a player could actually have top pair. It had never explicitly occurred to me, however, to deliberately make a list of those individual hands. Such a process, I thought, would have been excessively laborious and would accomplish nothing.

But Harrington's book now opened my eyes to a fundamental truth that would have a huge influence on my life from that point forward: A *category* of hand doesn't actually exist. And I then realized that listing the individual hands a category stood for *did* accomplish something—something very important. It plucked those categories out of the realm of empty abstractions, and brought them down to the level of concrete reality.

Thus, if there was an ace on the board and I asked the question, "what is the chance my opponent has top pair?" I would formerly visualize that abstract category only as a kind of floating, out of context ace. Then, I could only judge its probability by how often I had *seen* a player show down an ace in that situation. Of course, I couldn't say: "Out of the 84 times I have seen this type of situation, the opponent ended up having an ace in 23 of them." The human mind simply doesn't work that way. The best I could do was estimate that the opponent would "very often" have an ace in this situation, or "fairly often," or "only rarely," and so on. And even this would be of dubious accuracy.

But now that I could deliberately reduce these categories to individual hands, I acquired another way of answering this question. I could ask: "What would have physically needed to happen for my opponent to be holding an ace right now?" Or in other words: "Which individual, two-card hands with an ace in them could my opponent (if he was a good, rational player) have made all his preceding plays with?" Of course upon answering this question I would get the exact probability that he was holding an ace. And sometimes, I would even find that while the abstract category of top pair loomed large in my mind as a dangerous possibility, there were actually *no* two-card hands with which the opponent could feasibly have an ace under the present circumstances. This was one of the great benefits of reducing abstract categories to reality.

Though to be perfectly technical here, even individual hands are not yet *fully* reduced to reality. And I realized this at the time too. The most fundamental units of reality in a poker game are, really, the two-card combinations. After all, that is what *physically* happens in a poker game: Every player is dealt two unique plastic cards, each with a rank and a suit; and each combination has the exact same probability of being dealt as any other. Or to put it another way: The individual hand King-King is actually a *category* that contains the six separate combinations of K-K. And the category Ace-Jack contains two subcategories: A-J suited, which contains four separate combinations; and A-J offsuit, which contains twelve. Past that, things can be reduced no further: There is simply no such thing, in a game of Texas Hold'em, as a disembodied suit without a rank, or half a card, or a hand with only one card in it, and so forth.

Of course, Harrington's method absolutely *does* require reducing everything in the end to these combinations. But because in practice a player makes no distinction between hands like A♠-J♥ and A♠-J♦, the reduction to *individual hands* must be made logically, while the final reduction to *combinations* can be made mathematically.

It was, however, the idea of imagining myself in my opponent's position that amazed me most at the time. Specifically, it was the new role *experience* played in this approach that completely astounded me.

From reading Sklansky and other poker authors, I had long since accepted the idea that a large amount of *experience* was necessary to accurately read your opponents' hands. And indeed, as I played more and more poker, I did feel like I was getting better at it; only in a vague and indirect way. "Experience," as Sklansky meant it and as I used it at the time, meant the experience of seeing how *other people* played the game; which could then be used for estimating their hand frequencies.

But I now discovered that I possessed a completely different kind of experience: My own, personal, firsthand experience—not of how I saw other people play their hands, but of how I *knew* I would play my own.

Yet it was only after reducing hand categories to the reality they summarized that I became able to employ my experience in this way. After all, my firsthand experience is and can only be with reality— with individual hands.

If, for example, I asked myself how I would play *top pair* in my opponent's position, I would rarely be able to give a straight answer. After all, I would likely play different top pairs in different ways (depending on my second card). I would raise with some (like A-K), call with others (like A-T), and fold with still others (like A-3). It is only for *individual* hands that there is a definite correct play. And I now realized that in the vast majority of situations, I knew what that play was. *That* was the experience I had gained after playing and studying the game for two years.

But even after I reduced hand categories to individual hands, I couldn't *automatically* generate the entire range of these hands my opponent could have in a given situation. To do so, I actively had to visualize myself playing each individual hand in his position, and then compile the range out of that. I later noted that this was similar to the way most people do not explicitly know the order in which all the keys are arranged on a computer keyboard, yet are perfectly able to type on it and hit any key at will without looking. When they are given a pen, paper, and some time, however, most will be able to gradually reconstruct the keyboard by imagining themselves hitting each individual key and jotting down its position.

In an analogous way, by imagining myself playing in my opponent's stead, I was able to say how *I* would play each individual hand in his position, and know that it would be correct for him to make all the same plays as well.

(One problem with this, of course, was that I didn't know the correct play to make in *every* situation—otherwise, I wouldn't need to perform this analysis in the first place. I immediately realized I could solve this problem, however, by performing the same kind of analysis from my opponent's perspective. That is, I would analyze my own range of hands to determine the correct way for my opponent to play his. And this dovetailed perfectly with the need to employ deception, and to coordinate the way I would play all the hands in my range so that an observant opponent could not get a profitable read on me. It was only after this implementation that the "Structured Hand Analysis" method was really complete.)

And so, by applying just those two principles—(1) reducing hand categories to individual hands and (2) determining my opponent's possible hands using my own firsthand experience—every question and uncertainty I had about poker was instantly resolved. Suddenly, the entire decision-making process, which formerly consisted for me of one-half clear and logical mathematics, and the other half imprecise and experience-based *judgment*, became fused into a single comprehensive method: The whole of it clear, logical, mathematical.

I dealt out several more lab hands to further test this method, and was able to independently arrive at a clear, mathematical solution every time. I now made the momentous realization that once I ceased to think in categories, I no longer had to play according to categories either. And once I became able to rely on my own experience, I no longer had to rely on the experience of others.

THE DISCOVERY OF FREE-THINKING

This integration filled me with a real sense of enlightenment, of ecstasy, of deliverance. And the whole thing dawned on me not through any sort of gradual buildup, not as a series of progressive steps working up to a full understanding; but as a sudden explosion, an instantaneous series of insights that rocketed me straight out of a world of fog and uncertainty, and into one of utter clarity and understanding. Abraham Maslow (the great humanistic psychologist who coined the term self-actualization) would have undoubtedly labeled this a *peak-experience*.

I now sat completely still on my bed contemplating the implications of everything I had just discovered. My initial excitement had already subsided and was replaced by an extraordinary serenity. A bright, warm sensation washed over my body and became concentrated around my chest. My mind was greatly exalted; my thoughts were extremely clear, extraordinarily vivid.

My discovery, this alternate way of using experience and reasoning on the level of reality, was for me nothing less than an entirely new process of thinking; and a fundamentally *natural* one at that. It felt so profoundly *correct* to think this way, so natural, so rational, so *easy*. And when I did so, I became able to solve any poker problem that would have previously filled me with confusion and sent me searching through a stack of poker books to resolve.

The idea of "thinking for myself" — which I had often heard at school and on television before, and which I always brushed off as a bland truism — now popped into my mind and stood out in sharp clarity. This was undoubtedly it! And I became absolutely certain at that moment that it was precisely *this* kind of thinking that the human mind — with its abilities of learning from experience and of logical reasoning — was truly designed for. The term "free-thinking" occurred to me then as the most appropriate name for this new method of thought.

I was acutely aware, however, that this free-thinking was *not* some new skill I acquired through years of diligent training. It came to me as a sudden revelation. Within the span of an hour, although I had no clue of its existence before, the whole structure of this method rapidly unfolded itself and became firmly established in my mind. I concluded, therefore, that this free-thinking was in fact something I had been capable of all along. All I needed to do was realize that *this* was the way it had to be done. Indeed, it now seemed utterly self-evident to me that *this* was the way human beings were born to think: *For themselves,* on the basis of reality, and using their own firsthand experience and logic as their sole source of truth.

But that brought up the question: Why did it take me so long to realize this? And why didn't I have even an inkling that this kind of thought was possible before? The conclusion I reached at the time was that somewhere along the way I had lost something. Over many years of schooling and learning exclusively from teachers and books, analogous to the way I learned to play poker, I was taught to think and to act *categorically*. I had learned to always turn to someone else to tell me what was true, to tell me what was the correct way to do something, and I would always accept their word on the matter over my own judgment and experience. The ability to think for myself, I concluded, was killed off in me very early, nipped in the bud by my "education" before it had a chance to grow. And this to such a complete degree that until that very moment I wasn't even able to fathom what it meant. (It was only many years later that I would for the first time question these conclusions.)

In the meantime, however, I felt liberated. I knew that it was only by pure chance that I had broken free from the shackles of my categorical thinking, which I could have just as easily worn unwittingly for the rest of my life. I had an image of myself being thrown about for sixteen years by a dark, cold, turbulent ocean, when suddenly I was tossed out onto a warm, sunny island oasis; finally finding myself on firm ground, able to catch my breath, and knowing that I was now forever safe from being swept into that ocean again.

And so I sat on my bed musing, completely in awe of myself and everything I had just discovered, and how through a sheer burst of fortune I had unexpectedly stepped into the realm of *true thought* that was right and natural for man.

REAPING THE REWARDS

I don't remember what I did for the rest of that day, but from that moment forward I never opened another poker book again (that is, until eight years later, when I reread them all in order to write this current book).

I spent the ensuing weeks playing a lot of poker online; trying to perform a structured hand analysis on every hand I played, even if I already "knew" the correct way to play it. This wasn't restricted to No

Limit Hold'em either. I was fully able to apply the same method (of thinking in individual hands instead of categories and referring to my firsthand experience in determining the correct way to play them) to every single variation of poker—from Limit Hold'em, to Five-Card Draw, to Seven Stud Eight-or-Better. I found the process exhilarating.

A poker situation ceased to be merely a specific "item" that I needed to automatically—indeed almost robotically—match to one of a memorized set of categorical rules. Every decision suddenly became a unique problem, with its own unique determinants, all of which I had to dynamically take into account in order to arrive at the correct solution. Each hand was now a distinct challenge I had to meet—which I did very successfully. And I reaped the rewards of doing so in terms of money won at the poker table.

During this process, I had a chance to reexamine the categorical rules I formerly played by. Earlier, I accepted on the authority of various poker authors that these plays were correct, rationalizing to myself that the math behind them would work out, even though I had no way to check it. Now, of course, I had all the tools I needed to check it: to do the math in every hand myself, and see whether the plays these authors recommended really were correct. The results were extremely satisfying.

For some of the categorical plays I accepted on authority before, I could now see precisely *why* they were correct when I performed the Structured Hand Analysis. For other plays about which I was unsure, I was now able to separate the ones that were correct from the ones that weren't, and to find my own unique solutions to these (formerly) ambiguous problems. And for still a third group of plays, which I wholeheartedly accepted as correct on an author's authority, I now discovered that they were actually incorrect, and the math behind them simply *didn't* work out upon closer analysis. These I of course replaced with my own solutions.

It also became completely clear to me why it was inevitable that some of their plays would turn out incorrect. After all, if these poker authors were themselves categorical thinkers and were unable to perform the same kind of structured hand analysis (which according to their writings was undoubtedly the case), how were they to know what the correct plays in these situations really were? The answer is: They wouldn't, except by the same kind of intuitive estimates from experience I used to employ. But this is exactly what Harrington had said in his book all along:

> If you went to a poker tournament and posed [the] question [of how to play a specific hand] to a collection of good players, you'd get a bunch of reasonably informed opinions, based loosely on their experience over the years. . . . But when you were done, would you really know anything?
>
> Actually, you wouldn't. Guesswork, even informed guess-work from strong players, isn't the same as real knowledge. In poker, as in every other area of human endeavor, the considered opinions of a collection of the world's best practitioners might be right, but it might also be quite wrong. The consensus of what is considered true seems obvious and inevitable until some brave soul comes along and says "No, the truth is really like this."

And indeed, that is precisely what happened. Using structured hand analysis, I now became able to find my own answer to any poker problem and, as Harrington said, to "figure out things that no one else knows."

All this truly made me feel that I had reached a totally new level of poker-playing. And in fact, I really had!

There was, however, one major caveat I discovered about this method of Structured Hand Analysis: The fact that it was extremely mentally intensive, and ultimately very tiring. Every hand required a very precise and clear-headed process of thought, in which I had to keep my opponent's whole range of hands in short term memory and actively perform calculations on it in real time. Only when my mind was functioning at maximum efficiency could I successfully manage this task; and even then, it took all my mental resources to do so.

I discovered that I could only sustain this level of thought, at most, for one or two hours at a time. And afterwards I'd become very tired, my mind would begin working slower, and I couldn't keep all the necessary information in memory simultaneously. My hand analysis would then begin to get sloppy, I would start doing it only partially, and my calculations would be off. The result, of course, was that I would increasingly begin to make incorrect decisions, and would promptly have to leave the game before I hemorrhaged off all my money.

But this didn't bother me much. A couple of hours a day was plenty of time for me to play poker. I rarely played more than that even before. And my overall profits from the game had certainly increased tremendously.

A WIDER CONTEXT

Now, you may have been wondering: Why would I go into such an elaborate description of poker—including its technical aspects—in a book I intended to be a collection of biographies? Well, it is because this same fundamental experience—the discovery of free-thinking—was one that every single self-actualizing person I investigated had. It was invariably one of the most important, and often *the* most important experience of their lives—and is an indispensable part of self-actualization in general.

But while all of them *had* this experience, at different ages, in different contexts, and through different disciplines, none of them—and nobody else for that matter—ever described it in more than concise, cursory detail. My purpose has been to focus my own introspective microscope on this experience; to lay bare its most nuanced, intricate, microscopic psychological facets; and to in this way shed light on what took place in the minds of these great self-actualizers—but remained mostly unstated—during their own parallel realizations.

Appendix A: Two Approaches Any Problem

The following section is adapted from my larger book, *Self-Actualizing People in History*, and further elaborates on the difference between categorical thinkers and free-thinkers.

TOP-DOWN VERSUS BOTTOM-UP THINKING

There is a pair of terms, in memory psychology, that name two different modes of visual perception: "top-down" and "bottom-up" processing. There, bottom-up processing means looking at an object without the involvement of any prior knowledge—directly perceiving its individual details first, and making sense of the whole second. Top-down processing, in contrast, means visual perceiving *with* the involvement of prior knowledge—such as deliberately looking for an object of a particular type, and knowing what it should look like before you see it. A standard example is "looking *at* a flower, versus looking *for* a flower."

But this same schema, I realized, also applies to conscious, rational thinking—though in a somewhat different way.

For all disciplines, I would conclude years after my discovery of free-thinking, there exist two fundamentally different ways to approach any problem. The first may be called the categorical or *top-down* approach.

The person using this approach, before he is even confronted with a problem, must already know a number of preexisting categories into which that problem can fall, and a preordained method for solving each category of problem. When he does encounter a problem, he first identifies the larger category of problem to which it belongs, and only then applies the appropriate procedure for solving it. In other words, he approaches the problem from the *top* (his *general*, predetermined categories of problem) *down* (to the *specific* problem currently in front of him).

The second is the free-thinking or *bottom-up* approach. The person using this approach does not divide his discipline into multiple distinct categories of problem, but realizes that all individual problems in his discipline are merely variations of the *same* essential problem. This person first has to understand the most fundamental basis of his discipline, and grasp that every unique problem in it is made up of the same fundamental determinants differently combined. He will then understand that the solution of every problem is *inherent* in the very nature of his discipline—in the nature of the problems themselves and the goal their solution is intended to achieve. Granted this, he can then proceed to approach every problem individually, on its own basis, and solve it by an analysis of its most basic determinants.[43] In other words, he will approach each problem from the *bottom* (the *most basic* building-blocks of every problem in his discipline) up (to the *larger* problem he is currently confronted with).

But there is a crucial connection between these two seemingly separate methods of thinking: It is that categories do not come from nowhere! A category, after all, is a final conclusion. It is the product of a long process of thinking. Somebody had to do that thinking. Somebody had to form that conclusion. A category (if it is empirically valid) is the *result* of a bottom-up process of thinking, not separate from it. It is that thinking solidified into a rule.

The difference between the free-thinker and categorical thinker, then, is not that the latter uses the top-down and the former the bottom-up approach. It is that the exclusively categorical thinker, because he is psychologically incapable of bringing reality into the realm of logic, can *only* use the top-down approach. And since he is unable to

---

[43] Incidentally, the nature of the most basic, fundamental determinants — also call the "irreducible primaries" — of each discipline can vary enormously. (1) In math, these most basic fundamentals are logically given: they are postulated. (2) The irreducible fundamentals of poker — the two-card hands — are provided experientially: they are directly observable. (3) In science — such as organic chemistry — the fundamentals are neither logically given, nor directly observable: they must be *inferred* through scientific induction.

create his categories himself, there is only one place he can possibly get them: *from other people!* The free-thinker, by contrast, although he can also make use of the top-down approach, *he doesn't have to.* He is perfectly capable of approaching a problem from both sides, top-down *and* bottom-up. And the categories he uses are merely the condensations of his own bottom-up thinking.

Now as absurd as this may seem, there is certainly such thing as a categorical expert—in fact, these make up the vast majority of "experts" in nearly every discipline. Not knowing that bottom-up thinking is even possible, such a person invariably holds the belief that, within his discipline, there exist a variety of completely *separate* kinds of problem, and that he has to know and apply a completely separate technique for handling each one. Expertise for him means knowing and remembering a vast number of different and very specific *categories* of problem—the more numerous and specific the better—and having a separate, specialized tool for each. Skill to him means being able to choose from his entire collection of available categories the one that best fits each individual problem he is confronted with. His main difficulty is in dealing with novel problems, for which he has no predetermined category, and borderline cases, in which it is uncertain which of two (or more) categories a problem falls into.

Because he doesn't know that anything greater is possible, the categorical expert may often consider himself (and, even more often, *want* to consider himself) the best and most knowledgeable practitioner in his field. (That is precisely how I felt after playing Limit Hold'em categorically for two years, before I discovered Hand Analysis.) In this he is, of course, mistaken. It is only the free-thinking, bottom-up expert—what we may call the *true* expert—who can rightfully aspire to this title. Expertise to this person means knowing and understanding the fundamentals on which his discipline is based. Skill for him means the ability to deduce from these fundamentals the solution to any specific problem. His main difficulty is in actually making those deductions for each problem, which is a distinctly conscious and *dynamic* process requiring a substantial amount of time and effort.

A person can, of course, be a true, bottom-up expert in one discipline, but still a categorical thinker in many (or all) other areas of his life (like I was after discovering Structured Hand Analysis in poker, but before I expanded it to the rest of existence). And it is precisely by applying this same kind of *bottom-up* thinking to every area of his life—and specifically his personal, psychological life—that a person becomes fully self-actualizing.

A DEMONSTRATION OF THE ABOVE IN MATHEMATICS

The best and most relatable example of this—which I was aware of even in high school—is in the area of mathematics, where that distinction is plainly observable even among middle and high school students. Even as early as fifth or sixth grade (at least in schools with a respectable math curriculum), a line can be drawn between two types of math students: The *good* students, who understand the material and can solve each math problem (within their level of knowledge) bottom-up, and the *bad* students, who don't really understand the material, and must employ categorization to solve all the same problems.

When they are presented with a math problem, on a test for example, the *bad* students will first try to determine what *type* of problem it is and therefore what *equation* they must use to solve it. They will usually have all the equations perfectly memorized and know exactly which type of problem to apply which equation to: The Pythagorean equation for finding the sides of a right triangle, another equation for the sides of an isosceles triangle, another for finding the area of a circle, another if it is a problem of factoring, and so on and so forth. If these students fail to *identify* the problem and put it in the right category, they will inevitably use the wrong equation and arrive at the wrong answer.

The *good* math students on the other hand, when they are presented with the same problem, can approach it in a completely different way. Although they can also simply pick out the right equation to use (and usually this saves time) they do not *need* to. These students often don't have all of the necessary equations memorized, but given some time they can *re-derive* them.

Of course each complex math equation is *originally derived* from the combination of a few *more basic* equations, which are themselves ultimately derived from the most fundamental postulates of mathematics. The difference between the *good* math students and the *bad* ones is that the good students can once again re-derive those complex equations from their most basic premises (sometimes doing this many times over, since the ability to do so absolves them from having to commit those equations to memory), while the *bad* students (except maybe in a few simple instances) never can. This is because the *good* students truly *understand* those fundamental premises, how they relate to each other, and how they are logically built upon in the process of mathematics to create these much more complex *types* of math; while the bad students invariably don't.

Thus arise such absurdities as the bad students being able to follow a few simple rules of thumb to graph any parabola, circle, or other conic section from an $x = y$ equation, without knowing that the x and y actually stand for coordinates on a graph.

If the *good* students are presented with a new type of problem they haven't seen before, they will often be able to solve it using their knowledge and understanding of its more basic underlying concepts. The *bad* students can essentially *never* do this, except by accident — they have to learn how to deal with *that* type of problem separately.

Now in the classroom, the *bad* math students may get the same or even better grades than the *good* ones. Categorical mastery, after all, can go a long way. But when they are presented with more complex or more novel problems, they are likely to do *significantly* worse than the *good* students, who are able to deal with each problem from the bottom up, and come up with a solution without any prior familiarity with that exact *type* of problem.

It is also very telling, that the *bad* students nearly always end up hating math, finding it boring and frustrating, and doing it as a chore; while the *good* ones, who can really be said to *understand* it, usually enjoy it and may even come to *love* it.

Appendix B: Bruce Lee's "Style of No Style"

Bruce Lee (1940-1973) was a legendary, one-of-a-kind martial artist who achieved self-actualization. And he reached all the same conclusions I did about categorical and free-thinking, but in the discipline of martial arts.

Born to Chinese parents in 1940, Bruce spent his first eighteen years on the island of Hong Kong, where he learned—and became highly proficient at—the traditional Chinese kung fu style of Wing Chun. A true fighting prodigy, he later sought out and studied many additional martial arts styles—including other forms of kung fu, American boxing, fencing, karate, and judo—and incorporated many techniques from them into his own style.

Cleanly defeating every martial artist that challenged him, Bruce bragged that his traditional style of Wing Chun—which still formed the base of his fighting technique—was superior to all other styles. At age twenty-seven, however, he renounced the idea of martial art styles entirely, and founded his own martial arts school to which he gave the name Jeet Kune Do, and where he taught what he called "the style of no style."

When, years later, he was asked which fighting style was the most effective, he answered: "there is no such thing as an effective segment of a totality."

By that, I mean that I personally do not believe in the word style. Why? Because unless there are human beings with three arms and four legs, unless we have another group of beings on earth that are structurally different from us, there can be no different style of fighting. Why is that? Because we have only two hands and two legs. The most important thing is, how can we use them to the maximum?

There were, he would teach at his school, "three stages of cultivation" in the martial arts (and any endeavor in general). "The first stage," he said, "is the primitive stage."

It is a stage of original ignorance in which a person knows nothing about the art of combat. In a fight, he simply blocks and strikes instinctively without concern for what is right and wrong. Of course, he may not be so-called scientific, but, nevertheless, being himself, his attacks and defenses are fluid.

This was the stage Bruce Lee was at in his youth, when he got into countless street fights—nearly all of which he won—on the streets of Hong Kong, long before he started his training in martial arts. Here, the person fights wholly on instinct, emotion, and split-second judgment, and improves primarily through rote experience in unstructured fighting. It was also the stage I was at when I first started playing poker in school—also making decisions on instinct, emotion, and sporadic reasoning—before I picked up my first poker book. Unlike Bruce Lee, however, I stayed at that stage barely a month.

And he continues:

The second stage—the stage of sophistication, or mechanical stage—begins when a person starts his training. He is taught the different ways of blocking, striking, kicking, standing, breathing, and thinking. Unquestionably, he has gained the scientific knowledge of combat, but unfortunately his original self and sense of freedom are lost, and his action no longer flows by itself. His mind tends to freeze at different movements for calculations and analysis, and even worse, he might be called "intellectually bound" and maintain himself outside of actual reality.

This was Bruce Lee's stage after he began learning Wing Chun from his Chinese kung fu master, and my own stage after I started learning poker from books. It is a stage where, as Bruce Lee said, "you become all of a sudden a mechanical man," robotically following the formulas taught to you by others. But, as he pointed out, "formulas can only inhibit freedom, externally dictated prescriptions can only squelch creativity and assure mediocrity."

Then he described the final stage:

The third stage—the stage of artlessness, or spontaneous stage—occurs when, after years of serious and hard practice, the student realizes that after all, gung fu is nothing special. And instead of trying to impose on his mind, he adjusts himself to his opponent like water pressing on an earthen wall. It flows through the slightest crack. There is nothing to try [to] do but try to be purposeless and formless, like water. All of his classical techniques and standard styles are minimized, if not wiped out, and nothingness prevails. He is no longer confined.

This was the stage Bruce reached after he shucked his reliance on martial arts styles, and mine after I finally grasped Structured Hand Analysis. At this stage, as one Bruce Lee biographer summarized, the person has "thoroughly comprehended the universal principles that regulate all forms of combat." And these principles are, as Bruce stated, using your two arms and two legs to accomplish "the utmost" with the "minimum of movements and energy." Understanding this, the fighter "at the highest level of cultivation" knows that "circumstances must dictate what you do," and can dynamically adjust to the real situation and his current opponent. You "adapt to whatever the object is in front of you," Bruce said, summarizing the fundamental principles of fighting, "and the clumsier, the more limited the object, the easier it is for you to pot-shot it. That's what it amounts to!"

And once a person becomes capable of this, all of the fixed, separate, named categories of technique he learned over the years fall away too. "The best illustration" of this, said Bruce, "is something I borrowed from Ch'an (Zen):"

Before I studied the art, a punch to me was just a punch, a kick was just a kick. After I learned the art, a punch was no longer a punch, a kick no longer a kick. Now that I've understood the art, a punch is just a punch, a kick is just a kick.

And it is reaching this third stage of mastery in a discipline that is—as Bruce Lee well knew—a major milestone on the road to self-actualization (a term Bruce was highly familiar with, being as he was a contemporary of Abraham Maslow). It requires, Bruce Lee wrote, "doing one's best, dedicating one's self wholeheartedly to a given task, which happens to have no end but is an ongoing process." And "in my process," Bruce continued, describing his own psychological development, "I have changed from self-image actualization"—a term Bruce invented to mean putting on a façade, and choosing your words and your actions to project a false image of how you want others to see you—"to self-actualization, from blindly following propaganda, organized truths, etc., to search[ing] internally for the cause of my ignorance."[44]

SELF-TAUGHT MASTERY

This is of course a remarkable parallel to my own realization, but in a different discipline. There is, however, one thing I'd like to add to Bruce Lee's "three stages of cultivation" concept. It's that a person needs never go through the second, categorical stage at all.

These "three stages of cultivation" are really just *one* path to mastering martial arts (and many other disciplines). It is the path taken by those who seek out external instruction—from some teacher, or mentor, or expert. But there's also a second path: the independent one of the fully self-taught.

Though everyone starts at stage one—the "stage of original ignorance"—genuine improvement, through gained practice and experience, happens at that stage. Especially in physical disciplines—like

---

[44] One reason a dedicated, wholehearted pursuit of mastery in a discipline is so often found in the early lives of those individuals who later achieve self-actualization, is that it frequently leads to precisely this kind of epistemology experience—the discovery of free-thinking—which is an indispensable part of it. And the reason it does so, is simply because this "third stage" of mastery (or bottom-up approach) is objectively more effective than the "second stage" (the purely top-down approach). The individual genuinely dedicated to being the best he can be at some discipline, must therefore break through to this third stage if he's to achieve his goal. There's no guarantee he will reach this stage, but if he has the ability, and really is motivated by a love for his art, along with the drive to achieve excellence in it, he will succeed frequently enough.

fighting, tennis, soccer, and sports in general—a person's skill level will increase massively through sheer practice, practice, practice, in the complete absence of external guidance.

Most self-taught persons hit a ceiling with this, learning fundamentally bad habits and approaches that—if not unlearned—prevent them from improving past a certain level. There are, however, some totally self-taught prodigies who reach the highest level of competition in their chosen disciplines.

They do this not by remaining at the first "primitive stage," acting solely on instinct that has become second-nature to them from, let's say, hitting a tennis ball ten thousand times, with little to no regard for the theoretical underpinnings of their discipline. Rather, they arrive at a fundamental, first principles understanding of their discipline by means of their own firsthand experience, observation, and independent reasoning, thereby reaching the third stage without passing through the second.

Though these individuals do commonly invent their own concepts, techniques, categories, styles, and schools of thought, they do so independently, from the bottom up! Their categories, formulas, techniques, are just condensations of their own bottom-up process of thinking (a natural development in stage three), rather than handed-down snippets of wisdom from an external source, accepted on authority and without a full understanding (which is a wholly stage two phenomenon).[45]

It is true, however, that of those who reach the top level of competition in practically any discipline, the self-taught masters are

---

[45] I want to state this again, because it is such an important point: Employing categories, concepts, rules, techniques, and so on is not the antithesis of bottom-up, stage three, first-principles thinking—as Bruce Lee knew about fighting, I learned about poker, and any good mathematician who uses a formula he once derived knows about mathematics. It's indispensable for saving time, mental effort, and conveying information to other people. And the key distinction between stages two and three, is whether those categories are based on your own bottom-up thinking, or separate from it.

exceedingly rare. And the beginners that learn from a teacher or expert tend to improve many times faster—sometimes orders of magnitude faster—than those who remain self-taught. A single lesson with a top-level master, a wise saying goes, can be worth years of unstudied practice.

Appendix C: The Rules of Poker

As the now cliché saying goes, poker is a game that takes a few minutes to learn and a whole lifetime to master. So, here are the rules it only takes a few minutes to learn:

HAND RANKINGS

Poker is a card game played with a standard 52-card deck.[46] Each player is dealt a unique set of cards, and the players compete with each other for who will end up with the strongest hand. In all traditional forms of poker, a "hand" is a combination of five cards that can fall into one out of nine possible categories. These categories are ranked according to strength, and a higher-ranking category always beats a lower-ranking one. This makes "hand rankings" the first and most important aspect of the game that every beginner must learn.

The names of the nine categories of poker hand, ranked from the weakest to the strongest, are: (1) a High Card, (2) a Pair, (3) Two Pairs, (4) Three of a Kind, (5) a Straight, (6) a Flush, (7) a Full House, (8) Four of a Kind, and (9) a Straight Flush.

What five-card combination each of these categories requires is shown and explained below:

(9) Straight Flush:

A straight flush is five cards in sequential order and all of the same suit, such as:

---

[46] For those who don't know, a standard 52-card deck consists of four sets of thirteen sequentially ordered cards. The thirteen cards, ordered from highest to lowest, are: Aces, Kings, Queens, Jacks, Tens, Nines, Eights, Sevens, Sixes, Fives, Fours, Threes, and Twos. Each of the four sets of these thirteen cards comes in a different suit. The fours suits are: Spades ♠, Hearts ♥, Diamonds ♦, and Clubs ♣. Thirteen cards, each of four different suits, adds up to 13 multiplied by 4, which is 52 total cards.

[9♥] [8♥] [7♥] [6♥] [5♥]

If two or more players each have a straight flush, the one with the highest card in his five card sequence wins.

The four suits—spades♠, hearts♥, diamonds♦, and clubs♣—are all valued equally, and none is any stronger than the others.

The strongest possible straight flush is the Ace-high straight flush, consisting of an Ace, King, Queen, Jack, and Ten all of the same suit, which is also called a "Royal Flush."

And the lowest possible straight flush is the Ace-low straight flush, which consists of a Five, Four, Three, Two, and Ace, all of the same suit.

(8) Four of a Kind

A four of a kind is four cards of the same rank, and one additional side card, such as:

[8♠] [8♥] [8♣] [8♦] [J♥]

If two or more players each have a four of a kind, the one with the highest four of a kind wins.

And if two or more players each have the same four of a kind, the one with the highest side card wins.

(7) Full House

A full house is three cards of the same rank, plus two other cards of the same rank, such as:

[K♠] [K♣] [K♦] [2♥] [2♦]

If two or more players each have a full house, the one with the highest three of a kind wins.

And if two or more players each have a full house with the same three of a kind, the one with the highest adjoining pair wins.

(6) Flush

A flush is five cards all of the same suit, but not in sequential order like a royal flush, such as:

[Q♦] [8♦] [7♦] [5♦] [2♦]

If two or more players each have a flush, the one with the highest card in the flush wins.

And if two or more players each have a flush with the same highest card, then the second highest card — or, if that is the same, the third highest card (and then the fourth highest card, and then the fifth highest card) — becomes the deciding factor.

None of the four suits is ranked any higher than the others, and two otherwise identical flushes of two different suits are totally equal in value, and result in a draw between the two players.

(5) Straight

A straight is five cards in sequential order, but not all of the same suit, such as:

[7♣] [6♦] [5♣] [4♣] [3♥]

If two or more players each have a straight, the one with the highest card in the sequence wins.

And if two or more players each have a straight with the same highest card, the hand results in a draw and they split all the chips in the pot.

An Ace may be used as the highest card in an Ace-high straight (A-K-Q-J-T) or as the lowest card in a five-high straight (5-4-3-2-A).

(4) Three of a Kind

A three of a kind is three cards of the same rank, plus two non-pairing cards of a different rank, such as:

[J♠] [J♥] [J♦] [8♣] [3♦]

If two or more players each have a three of a kind, the one with the highest three of a kind wins.

And if two or more players each have the same three of a kind, the one with the highest fourth card—and, if that is the same, with the highest fifth card—wins.

(3) Two Pair

A two pair is a pair of cards of the same rank, plus another pair of cards of a different rank, and a fifth side card which doesn't match either, such as:

[T♣] [T♦] [4♠] [4♣] [9♥]

If two or more players each have a two pair, the one with the highest pair—and, if that is the same, the one with the highest second pair—wins.

And if two or more players each have the same two pair, the one who holds the highest fifth card wins.

(2) Pair

A pair is two matching cards of the same rank, plus three non-matching cards of different ranks, such as:

[A♠] [A♥] [J♠] [6♠] [2♥]

If two or more players each have a pair, the one with the highest pair wins.

And if two or more players each have the same pair, the one with the highest third card—and, if that is the same, with the highest fourth card; and, if that is the same, with the highest fifth card—wins.

(1) High Card

A high card is five non-matching cards, all of different ranks, not all in sequential order, and not all of the same suit, such as:

[K♠] [T♠] [8♥] [6♦] [3♥]

This is the weakest category of hand a player can have.

If two or more players each have only a high card, the one with the highest card—followed by the highest second card, followed by the highest third card, and so on—wins.

RULES OF TEXAS HOLD'EM

The above five-card hand rankings are universal across all traditional forms of poker. But since in this book we're only discussing one form of poker, Texas Hold'em, only the rules to this game are included here.

THE FIVE STAGES OF A HOLD'EM HAND

Preflop

All Texas Hold'em games start with anywhere between the minimum two and the maximum ten players sitting at a poker table. A hand begins with each player being dealt two cards facedown, which he alone is able to look at—these cards belong solely to him, and are called his "hole cards." This is the first of five total stages in a dealt hand, called the "preflop" stage.

The Flop
Then, if more than one player remains after this first stage, the hand moves on to its second stage called the "flop." On the flop, three "community" cards are dealt face-up in the middle of the table. These cards belong to all players, and each one can use them in combination with her two "hole" cards to build the best five-card poker hand she can.

The Turn
Then, if more than one player remains after the flop, the hand proceeds to its third stage known as the "turn." Here an additional, fourth community card is dealt face-up in the middle of the table, which can again be used by all the players to build their five-card combinations.

The River
Then, if more than one player remains after the turn, the game moves to its fourth stage called the "river." On the river, the fifth and final community card is dealt face-up on the board, leaving each player with two hidden hole cards and five common community cards, for a total of seven. Out of these seven, each player has to choose five—any five—to make the best five-card combination available to him.

The Showdown
Then, if more than one player remains to the end of the river, those who remain flip up their two hidden cards to see who has the best five-card hand. This finale is called the "showdown." And the player who shows down the strongest five-card combination ends up winning that hand, and takes all the money he and the other players put in the pot over the course of that hand (the part about money is explained in the next section).

Texas Hold'em is winner-takes-all, and there is no prize for the second-best hand. In the event of a draw, the pot is split evenly between the two or more players tied for the winning hand.

BETTING

Poker is a game played with money, or "chips" that represent money. To play, each player sitting down at the poker table must buy-in for a certain about of money—let's say a minimum of two hundred dollars. Players then use this money to make wagers, or "bets," against one another.

As he tries to make the best five-card hand, each player can basically bet with the other players that his hand is actually the best one, or will end up being the best one after all the cards have been dealt. The other players can believe this assertion, and throw away—or "fold"—their hands without accepting the bet, and thus allow the bettor to win the hand (and all the bets already made in it up to that point), whether he really did hold the best cards or not. They can also accept the bet, or "call," and see which one of them really does have the best hand. And they can bet even more money, or "raise," essentially claiming that they, and not the original bettor, possess the superior holdings.

The player who shows down the best five-card hand, or gets all his opponents to throw away their hands before the showdown, ends up winning all of the bets made by all of the players during that hand.

The Four Rounds of Betting

There are four rounds of betting in a Texas Hold'em hand: (1) the pre-flop round, after the first two cards are dealt; (2) the flop round, after the first three community cards are dealt; (3) the turn round, after the fourth community card has been dealt; and (4) the river round, after the last community card is dealt. There is no more betting after the showdown.

The Pot

At the end of each betting round, all the money bet by the players during that round is pooled together, and added to a common fund at the center of the table known as the "pot." The whole pot is ultimately awarded to the winner of the hand.

The Blinds

A Hold'em hand starts, before the first two cards are even dealt to each player, with two of the players forced to put in an automatic bet: a full-sized bet, called the "big blind," and a half-sized bet, called the "small blind." These bets are called "blinds," of course, because the players put them in blind without seeing their cards.

In every Hold'em game, the blind sizes are fixed at a set amount—let's say $10 for the big blind, and $5 for the small blind. The player who must put in, or "post," the small blind is always the player who sits directly to the right of the player posting the big blind. At the end of each hand, the players required to post the big and small blinds shift one position to the left—so that, after one circle around the table, the burden of posting the blinds falls on all players equally.

Betting Choices: Fold, Call, or Raise

Once the blinds are posted and the hole cards dealt, the betting action moves clockwise around the poker table, starting with the player sitting to the left of the big blind. This player must make a decision, one of just three possible decisions that exist in poker: to fold, to call, or to raise.

Folding means not accepting the current bet, and throwing away one's hand without putting in any more money. Calling means accepting the current bet, and putting in whatever amount of money is needed to match it. And raising means not only matching the current bet, but putting in even more money (the allowed amount depending on whether you're playing Limit or No Limit Hold'em), thus increasing the current bet size, and becoming the bettor oneself.

Calling when the current bet is zero is called "checking." And raising when the current bet is zero is simply called "betting."

Betting Sizes: Limit and No Limit Hold'em

In Limit Hold'em, the bet sizes are fixed in relation to the blinds, and raising occurs in increments. The amount any player can raise is limited to one times (1x) the big blind, on top of the current bet, during the preflop and flop rounds; and doubles to two times (2x) the big blind, on top of the current bet, during the turn and the river rounds.

In No Limit Hold'em, each player can raise any amount, from a minimum double the size of the current bet (or just one big blind if the current bet is zero), up to all of the money he has in front of him. Other than that, the rules to Limit and No Limit Hold'em are identical.

Stacks, Side Pots, and Being All-In

During a poker hand, no player can lose more money than he has in front of him. This money is known as his "stack" (short for his "stack of chips"), and is the total amount he has available to make raises and calls with. Although each player must buy in for a minimum amount, let's say $200, after losing a few hands, his stack might be reduced to just $50 or $10.

If he has less money in front of him than is needed for calling the current bet or making the minimum raise, these actions will put him "all-in." This means he puts in the remainder of his money, and then keeps his hole cards until the showdown, but without being able to take further actions during that hand.

He's also eligible to win only the bets made prior and up to his "all-in" move, assuming he shows down the best hand after the river; and any money the other players put in on top of that will go to a separate "side pot" contested between them.

For example: If a player faces a $20 bet on the turn, and he only has $5 left in front of him, he is able to call that bet with his last $5, and be placed all-in. He can, however, win only the money already in the "main pot" from the preflop and flop betting rounds, plus $5 more from each player who matched that $20 bet on the turn. But he can't win the remaining three-fourths of that $20 bet from any of the players, nor any additional bets they will make on the turn or river. That money is put in a separate side pot, which goes to whomever shows down the best hand among the still active players (or folds out all of them but himself), even if he loses the main pot by having a worse five-card hand than the all-in player.

Betting Action

Preflop, after the first player sitting directly left of the big blind makes his decision to fold, call, or raise, the action moves to the next player to his left. Then that player makes his decision to fold, call, or raise, followed by the next player to his left, and so on and so forth, until the action makes its way back to the big blind.

A betting round only ends when all active players—those who haven't folded and aren't all in—have acted at least once (posting the blind isn't considered an action), and have all put in the same quantity of money equal to the current bet. If one player raises, the betting action starts all over again, until all other players responded to his raise. Then, if those players just fold to or call his raise, the betting round ends, and the hand will proceed to the next stage. If someone else raises, however, he restarts the betting action once more, and all other players now have to respond to his raise.

In Limit Hold'em, the maximum number of raises allowed on a betting round is four: three raises and one initial bet. After the fourth raise, the only remaining options are calling or folding, so all rounds will eventually end after no more than four circles around the table.

Betting Order

There exist three key positions in every Hold'em Hand: the big blind, the small blind, and the player sitting right of the small blind, known as the "button."[47] In games with just two players, the small blind is also the button. These positions dictate the betting order on each round.

On the preflop round, the player left of the big blind is always the first to act, and—unless someone else raises—the big blind is last to act. On all other rounds—flop, turn, and river—the closest player sitting left of the button is always the first to act; and, unless someone

---

[47] Button is short for "dealer button," because in home games where there was no separate dealer, that was the player who dealt out the cards for that hand. There was, and in all proper Hold'em games still is, a real plastic button the size of a poker chip, indicating who the dealer for that hand was (or would have been).

else raises, the button—or, if she folded, the closest player sitting right of the button—is always the last to act. This order remains constant, no matter what happened on previous betting rounds.

Showdown Order

During the showdown, the order the players must turn up their cards in is also exactly the same. The closest player left of the button is first to reveal his hand; and the button—or, if she folded, the next closest player sitting right of the button—is always the last.

If every player before him turns over a hand he can tie with or beat, the next player *must* show his hole cards, or surrender all claims to the pot. But if any player before him shows down a hand that beats his, the next player now has the option to throw his cards out without showing, also called "mucking" his hand, without revealing the actual hand he lost with.

****

And that's it! You now know the complete rules to Texas Hold'em: a deceptively simple game that takes minutes to learn, and decades to master.

Works Cited

Ciaffone, Bob, and Jim Brier. *Middle Limit Holdem Poker*. Bob Ciaffone, 2001.

Harrington, Dan, and Bill Robertie. *Harrington on Hold'em : Expert Strategy for No-Limit Tournaments. Vol. 1, Strategic Play*. Henderson, NV, Two Plus Two Publishing. 2004.

---. *Harrington on Hold'em: Expert Strategy for No-Limit Tournaments. Vol. 2, The Endgame*. Henderson, NV, Two Plus Two Publishing, 2004.

---. *Harrington on Hold'em: Expert Strategy for No-Limit Tournaments. Vol. 3, The Workbook*. Henderson, NV, Two Plus Two Publishing, 2006.

Kahneman, Daniel. *Thinking, Fast and Slow*. New York, Farrar, Straus And Giroux, 2013.

Little, John R. *The Warrior Within : The Philosophies of Bruce Lee to Better Understand the World around You and Achieve a Rewarding Life*. New York, Mcgraw-Hill, 1996.

Miller, Ed, David Sklansky, and Mason Malmuth. *Small Stakes Hold'em: Winning Big With Expert Play*. Henderson, NV, Two Plus Two Publishing, 2004.

Rand, Ayn, and Peter Schwartz. *Return of the Primitive : The Anti-Industrial Revolution*. New York, Meridian Book, 1999.

Sklansky, David. *The Theory of Poker: A Professional Poker Player Teaches You How To Think Like One*. Fourth ed., Henderson, NV, Two Plus Two Publishing, 1999.

Sklansky, David, and Mason Malmuth. *Hold'em Poker for Advanced Players*. Henderson, NV, Two Plus Two Publishing, 2005.

Sklansky, David, and Ed Miller. *No Limit Hold'em: Theory and Practice*. Henderson, NV., Two Plus Two Publishing, 2007.

Abbreviations:

HoH1 - Harrington, Dan, and Bill Robertie. *Harrington on Hold'em, Vol. 1*

HoH2 - Harrington, Dan, and Bill Robertie. *Harrington on Hold'em, Vol. 2*

HoH3 - Harrington, Dan, and Bill Robertie. *Harrington on Hold'em, Vol. 3*

HPAP - Sklansky, David and M. Malmuth. *Hold'em Poker for Advanced Players*

MLHP - Ciaffone, Bob, and Jim Brier. *Middle Limit Holdem Poker*

SSH - Miller, Ed, David Sklansky, and Mason Malmuth. *Small Stakes Hold'em*

ToP - Sklansky, David. *The Theory of Poker*

WoW - Little, John R. *The Warrior Within*

Notes:

"the method by which..." Rand, Ayn, et al. *Return of the Primitive*, p 55

"We believe that this book..." *MLH*, p 4

"Whatever your level of play..." ToP, p 2

"This book picks up where..." SSH, p 5

"In Texas hold'em it is relatively..." HPAP, p 49

Starting hand requirements chart - SSH, pp 80-81

"If you are new to hold'em..." HPAP, p 5

"These recommendations are not rigid..." SSH, p 76

"View them like training wheels..." SSH, p 76

"An expert player who fully..." SSH, p 76

"After the first round..." HPAP, p 52

"Which is why it's important..." HPAP, p 52

"A $30-$60 game. You are in the big blind..." MLH, p 97

"impart the general principles of..." MLH, p 1

"Proper play on the turn..." MLH, pp 148-149

"A $15-$30 game. You raise from..." MLH, pp 165-166

"A $15-$30 game. You are on the button..." MLH, pp 163-164

"A $30-$60 game. You are on the button..." MLH, p 251

"To win at poker..." SSH, p 23

"Money does not appear..." SSH, p 20

"All poker starts as..." ToP, p 27

"If everybody's cards were..." ToP, p 17

"Of course, if all cards..." ToP, p 17

"Poker, like all card games..." ToP, p 17

"There are two important..." SSH, 26-27

"When you compute odds..." ToP, p 50

"Figuring effective odds may... You add all the calls" ToP, p 53

"If you have ace-king..." SSH, p 27

"The art of poker..." ToP, p 17

"If your opponents all played..." SSH, p 16

"Your edge comes not..." ToP, p 15

"In hold'em, any time an..." ToP, p 205

"You analyze the meaning..." HPAP, p 225

"put[ting] these two pieces..." HPAP, p 225

"In other words, you use logic..." HPAP, p 225

"Reading hands is both... It is an art..." ToP, p 221

"Determine the possible hands..." ToP, p 248

"put an opponent on a..." HPAP, p 225

"There is almost no question..." HPAP, p 153

"But you will not win..." HPAP, p 153

"Your opponent, who is a good... Should you check..." ToP, p 250

"think of the various hands..." ToP, p 250

"Your opponent could be slowplaying..." ToP, pp 250-251

"Opponent's Possible Hands" diagram - ToP, p 252

"You know that if you bet... Therefore, after your opponent..." ToP, p 251

"Because you expect your..." ToP, p 252

"When all the cards are out..." ToP, p 35

"Hand reading is also..." Sklansky, David, et al. *No Limit Hold'em*, p 15

"Basically, there are only two..." MLH, p 20

"As your opponents get tougher..." ToP, p 222

"Imagine that you are…" ToP, pp 165-166

"Mathematically, optimal bluffing…" ToP, pp 166

"You are on the button with…" SSH, p 271

"You have J♥5♦ in the big…" SSH, pp 295-296

"squeeze every last penny…" SSH, p 5

"in hold'em, an almost infinite…" HPAP, p 110

"Working through these…. You will encounter…" SSH, p 256

"Your first job is to…" HoH3, p 18

"If you had one of…" HoH3, p 225

"We know there are 1,326…. Once two cards are removed…" HoH2, p 165

"With Queens … reraise 70%..." HoH1, p 190

"Harrington's Law of Bluffing…" HoH1, p 61

"Structured Hand Analysis…" HoH2, p 163

"If this seems like an…" HoH1, p 136

"And if you ever wondered…" HoH1, p 136

"If you went to a poker…" HoH2, p 162

"figure out things that…" HoH2, p 163

"there is no such thing as… By that, I mean…" WoW, p 106-107

"The first stage is the… It is a stage of original ignorance…" WoW, p 108

"The second stage — the stage of…" N/a WoW, p 109

"you become all of a sudden…" WoW, p 124

"formulas can only inhibit…" WoW, p 113

"The third stage — the stage of…" WoW, p 109

"thoroughly comprehended the universal…" WoW, p 112

"the utmost" with the "minimum of movements…" WoW, p 119

"at the highest level of cultivation… circumstances must…" WoW, p 164

"adapt to whatever the object … and the clumsier…" WoW, p 119

"The best illustration…. Before I studied the art…" WoW, p 119

"doing one's best, dedicating…" WoW, p 133

"in my process… "I have changed from self-image…" WoW, pp 133, 128

CPSIA information can be obtained
at www.ICGtesting.com
Printed in the USA
LVHW011827140720
660691LV00012B/1091